DREAMS AND VISIONS FROM MY HEAVENLY FATHER

A Story of Grace and
Divine Inheritance

Becky Blankenship

authorHOUSE®

AuthorHouse™
1663 Liberty Drive
Bloomington, IN 47403
www.authorhouse.com
Phone: 1 (800) 839-8640

Published by AuthorHouse   02/21/2017

ISBN: 978-1-5246-5842-7 (sc)
ISBN: 978-1-5246-5841-0 (e)

Print information available on the last page.

Any people depicted in stock imagery provided by Thinkstock are models, and such images are being used for illustrative purposes only. Certain stock imagery © Thinkstock.

This book is printed on acid-free paper.

"I (God) have wiped out your transgressions like a thick cloud and your sins like a heavy mist. Return to Me, for I have redeemed you."

Isaiah 44:22 (Amplified Bible)

[11] "For I know the plans I have for you," declares the LORD, "plans to prosper you and not to harm you, plans to give you hope and a future."

Jeremiah 29:11 (NIV)

[38] For I am convinced that neither death, nor life, nor angels, nor principalities, nor things present, nor things to come, nor powers, [39] nor height, nor depth, nor any other created thing, will be able to separate us from the love of God, which is in Christ Jesus our Lord.

Romans 8:38-39 (NASB)

CONTENTS

FOREWORD

I write this book in hopes that each and every person who reads the words on the following pages will be touched and encouraged, no matter what faith, or no faith, you hold in your heart. We are all on this journey of life together, with the good and the bad all mixed into it, walking day by day, whether we admit it or not, affecting some other life or lives on this planet for good or for bad.

It is my deep desire and passion that something you read here will be the catalyst that will spur you onto the great things that you're supposed to do in life, to fulfill the dreams and visions that have been planted in your heart no matter how long they've been sitting there unreached, to stretch toward the high calling assigned to the uniqueness that is you and you alone on this path we all trod.

DEDICATION

I dedicate this book to my wonderful husband Randy who has stuck by me through the good times and the tough ones. Thank you for all these 40 years of marriage in which you have worked harder than anyone I know, helping thousands of people successfully navigate their way to resolution of their legal problems in so many varied areas of concern.

You are undoubtedly the "Best Boss Ever" as dear Linda and Angel love to say, as well as an excellent loving and faithful husband, father to our daughters Beth and Grace, father-in-law to Nick and Xavier, and Granddad to our precious grandsons Finn and Miles and to any and all future grandkids.

Your knowledge of God's Word has inspired so many as you have taught countless Sunday School classes to our friends over the last 30 years. God has used you mightily, Randy, and I am so blessed to be your wife on this journey. Thank you with all of my heart for the love, the support and the encouragement you have given me to follow my vision in writing this book. I love you. Becky

HOW THIS BOOK CAME TO BE

Why this book? That is surely a very good question, for I have never before written a book. Now I do send out a weekly email to our Sunday School class with a word of encouragement from God's Word to all those who are members, or have been in the past. These emails include praise reports of answered prayers and prayer requests for challenging situations, but other than that, I am a novice at this.

I have over the past 40 years spent many countless hours poring over the treasures in God's Word, the Bible, hiding the verses in my heart in preparation to pray more effectively for many, many loved ones and even perfect strangers who are in need. During this process I have had the honor and blessing of receiving dreams and visions which I believe are from the Lord, and have shared them with my friends. These dear sisters in the Lord have encouraged me many times to write them all down and put them into book form, thus, "Dreams and Visions from My Heavenly Father, a Story of Grace and Divine Inheritance" came to be.

I have not asked for these dreams and visions, but believe that this may be one of the many methods God has used over the centuries to speak to people, almost like watching a video in your mind, all of it based upon the Word of God, the Bible, and Its Promises.

As for the title of this book, The Lord and I have gone round and round about that many, many times. You may be familiar with a well-known best seller, "Dreams From My Father, a Story of Race and Inheritance," by a very well known author, Barack Hussein Obama. I truly have not had, and believe me, still do not have any intentions of comparing this book with his, or of competing with his writing skills, however, this is the title I have heard over and over each time I have prayed about it as I have typed these dreams and visions onto the page.

I remember reading something so powerful about the well-known evangelist Billy Graham that profoundly affected my life. Someone asked him how, in light of the many Christian evangelists who have fallen over the past decades, he had kept himself free from scandal and had maintained such a powerful ministry throughout the entire world. He answered that wherever he goes he ALWAYS takes His Bible with him and keeps it laid open so that whatever block of time he has available to him, he spends it reading what God has shown him through His Word. To that I say, "Wow!" I'm not there by any stretch of the imagination, but what a goal to shoot for. The evidence is clear through the effects of Billy Graham's life and the vision and ministry God has given him to fulfill with that totally submitted life. In Hebrews 4:12 (NIV) it states, that the Word of God is "alive and powerful, and sharper than any two-edged sword; able to divide between soul and spirit, even down to the joints and marrow of the bones; and able to judge and discern the very thoughts and intentions of our hearts." Why wouldn't we spend the time it takes to change us from the inside out, to prepare us for the battles of life, to help others in need with the Wisdom only God can give, and to be open to whatever means He chooses to do so.

In preparing for this book I felt compelled to research the actual word "vision" and the ways it is used in the Bible, and I would like to share those with you now.

Webster's Dictionary defines **vision** as

n. 1. The act of seeing external objects; actual sight.
    Faith here is turned into vision there.- Hammond.

2. *(Physiol.)* The faculty of seeing; sight; one of the five senses, by which colors and the physical qualities of external objects are appreciated as a result of the stimulating action of light on the sensitive retina, an expansion of the optic nerve.

3. That which is seen; an object of sight.

4. Especially, that which is seen otherwise than by the ordinary sight, or the rational eye; a supernatural, prophetic, or imaginary sight; as, the visions of Isaiah.
    No dreams, but visions strange-Sir P. Sidney

And now as you will see in the following references from the New International Version, God has used dreams and visions to impact men and women's lives, as well as whole nations throughout history.

The Lord's Covenant with Abram

Genesis 15:1-12, 17-18 (NIV)--15 After this, the word of the LORD came to Abram in a **vision**: "Do not be afraid, Abram. I am your shield, your very great reward." [2] But Abram said, "Sovereign LORD, what can you give me since I remain childless and the one who will inherit my estate is Eliezer of Damascus?" [3] And Abram said, "You have given me no children; so a servant in my household will be my heir." [4] Then the word of the LORD came to him: "This man will not be your heir, but a son who is your own flesh and blood will be your heir." [5] He took him outside and said, "Look up at the sky and count the stars—if indeed you can count them." Then he said to him, "So shall your offspring be." [6] Abram believed the LORD, and he credited it to him as righteousness.

[7] He also said to him, "I am the LORD, who brought you out of Ur of the Chaldeans to give you this land to take possession of it." [8] But Abram said, "Sovereign LORD, how can I know that I will gain possession of it?" [9] So the LORD said to him, "Bring me a heifer, a goat and a ram, each three years old, along with a dove and a young pigeon." [10] Abram brought all these to him, cut them in two and arranged the halves opposite each other; the birds, however, he did not cut in half. [11] Then birds of prey came down on the carcasses, but Abram drove them away. [12] **As the sun was setting, Abram fell into a deep sleep, and a thick and dreadful darkness came over him**. [17] When the sun had set and darkness had fallen, a smoking firepot with a blazing torch appeared and passed between the pieces. [18] On that day the LORD made a covenant with Abram and said, "To your descendants I give this land, from the Wadi of Egypt to the great river, the Euphrates.

God's Vision for and Blessing upon Ishmael

Genesis 17:20 (NIV)-- [20] And as for Ishmael, I have heard you: I will surely bless him; I will make him fruitful and will greatly increase his numbers.

The Lord spoke in a vision to his people to tell them of his anointing on David:

Psalm 89:18-20 (NIV)--**¹⁸** Indeed, our shield belongs to the Lord, our king to the Holy One of Israel. ¹⁹ **Once you spoke in a vision, to your faithful people** you said: "I have bestowed strength on a warrior; I have raised up a young man from among the people. ²⁰ I have found David my servant; with my sacred oil I have anointed him.

The Promise of Israel's Return

Ezekiel 11:14-25 (NIV)--¹⁴ The word of the Lord came to me: ¹⁵ "Son of man, the people of Jerusalem have said of your fellow exiles and all the other Israelites, 'They are far away from the Lord; this land was given to us as our possession.' ¹⁶ "Therefore say: 'This is what the Sovereign Lord says: Although I sent them far away among the nations and scattered them among the countries, yet for a little while I have been a sanctuary for them in the countries where they have gone.' ¹⁷ "Therefore say: 'This is what the Sovereign Lord says: I will gather you from the nations and bring you back from the countries where you have been scattered, and I will give you back the land of Israel again.'¹⁸ "They will return to it and remove all its vile images and detestable idols. ¹⁹ I will give them an undivided heart and put a new spirit in them; I will remove from them their heart of stone and give them a heart of flesh. ²⁰ Then they will follow my decrees and be careful to keep my laws. They will be my people, and I will be their God. ²¹ But as for those whose hearts are devoted to their vile images and detestable idols, I will bring down on their own heads what they have done, declares the Sovereign Lord."

²² Then the cherubim, with the wheels beside them, spread their wings, and the glory of the God of Israel was above them. ²³ The glory of the Lord went up from within the city and stopped above the mountain east of it. ²⁴ **The Spirit lifted me up and brought me to the exiles in Babylonia in the vision given by the Spirit of God. Then the vision I had seen went up from me, ²⁵ and I told the exiles everything the Lord had shown me.**

Here's something to seriously consider: God's perfect timing in fulfilling visions.

Ezekiel 12:26-28 (NIV)--²⁶ The word of the LORD came to me: ²⁷ "Son of man, the Israelites are saying, '**The vision he sees is for many years from now, and he prophesies about the distant future.**' ²⁸ "Therefore say to them, 'This is what the Sovereign LORD says: None of my words will be delayed any longer; whatever I say will be fulfilled, declares the Sovereign LORD.'"

God is seated on the throne in Heaven. He KNOWS all things, and assuredly knows WHEN to bring His Word to pass in every matter, in every life. We've got to be open to His revelation of His Plans.

In Habakkuk 2:1-3 (AMP), God speaks so powerfully through the prophet Habakkuk saying:

"I will stand at my guard post and station myself on the tower; and I will keep watch to see what He will say to me, and what answer I will give [as His spokesman] when I am reproved.

² Then the LORD answered me and said, "**Write the vision and engrave it plainly on tablets so that the one who reads it will run**. ³ "**For the vision is yet for the appointed [future] time. It hurries toward the goal [of fulfillment]; it will not fail. Even though it delays wait [patiently] for it, because it will certainly come; it will not delay.**

And yet how many of us have, in the discouragement of delay, given up on our dreams and visions because time has diluted our determination and has wilted our faith to believe they would come to pass? Proverbs 29:18 boldly speaks this truth which is the state of so many today: ¹⁸ "**Where there is no vision, the people perish**." They don't just fall down and can't get up....they perish!!!

This is serious business, brothers and sisters!!! We must be equipped with God's Word to be the Barnabbas, the Encourager, to those who are on the verge of giving up on their dreams and visions.

Read what the Lord spoke about the prophet Samuel in 1 Samuel 3:19 "And Samuel grew, and the Lord was with him, **and did let none of his words fall to the ground."** As Jehovah filled this man of God with supernatural power to bring His Words to pass, we must be the ones to hold each other up in prayer that is fed by the eternal Power of God's Promises. Thus, the words, the dreams and visions that God Almighty has given to His children will also come to pass, and not one of them will fall to the ground, fruitless and unfulfilled, but full of the Power of our Creator Himself Who spoke the worlds into existence by the very Word of His Power.

In Acts 2: 14, 16-21(KJV), the Apostle Peter boldly declared God's Word taken from Joel: ¹⁴ "But Peter, standing up with the eleven, lifted up his voice, and said unto them, Ye men of Judaea, and all ye that dwell at Jerusalem, be this known unto you, and hearken to my words: ¹⁵ For these are not drunken, as ye suppose, seeing it is but the third hour of the day. ¹⁶ But this is that which was spoken by the prophet Joel: ¹⁷ And it shall come to pass in the last days, saith God, "**I will pour out of my Spirit upon all flesh: and your sons and your daughters shall prophesy, and your young men shall see visions, and your old men shall dream dreams.** ¹⁸ And on my servants and on my handmaidens I will pour out in those days of my Spirit; and they shall prophesy: ¹⁹ And I will shew wonders in heaven above, and signs in the earth beneath; blood, and fire, and vapour of smoke. ²⁰ The sun shall be turned into darkness, and the moon into blood (have you seen the Blood Moons?), before the great and notable day of the Lord come. ²¹ **And it shall come to pass, that whosoever shall call on the name of the Lord shall be saved.**" THAT IS GOOD NEWS, and we can all be a part of its fulfillment!!!

And the Good News at the end of Proverbs 29:18 which you read earlier is this: **"but he that keepeth the law, happy is he!"** That's what we're talking about, people who have heard and seen what God's Plan is for their lives, who stay the course, who hide God's Word in their hearts and speak it forth in faith, people who believe to the end of their dream or vision, HAPPY ARE THEY!!! That's why I'm writing this book! It's for you to keep on keeping on and not to give up on the dreams and visions God has revealed to you. YOU **CAN** DO IT!!! **WE** CAN DO IT....TOGETHER!!!

THE HAMMER AND THE FIRE

In Jeremiah 23:28-29 (NKJV) God's Word tells us this: "²⁸ **The prophet that has a dream, let him tell a dream; and he that has My Word, let him speak My Word faithfully**. What is the chaff to the wheat?" says the LORD. ²⁹ **"Is not My Word like as a fire?" says the LORD, "and like a hammer that breaks the rock in pieces?"**

As I have spent many hours and years in prayer for people over the years, I have always been drawn to the part of the above scripture that asks the question, "Is not My Word like as a fire?" says the Lord, "and like a hammer that breaks the rock in pieces?"

What I believe the Lord showed me concerning this verse is this: Is there a person in your life who seems to be cold and hard against the things the Lord is trying to accomplish in his or her life? Have you prayed for years for this person, including yourself, with seemingly no success? Then, "Hide My Word in your heart;" "Put Me in remembrance of My Word," says the Lord Who is "not willing that any should perish, but for all to come to repentance," and to live the abundant life Jesus promised His followers.

I remember many years ago attending a series of meetings at the church we attended at the time, in which a man who was a well-known Christian speaker and author spoke each night in a way I had never heard anyone speak. It was as if the Words of the Bible were his native language. Scripture just flowed out of his mouth like a river; beautiful, power-filled verse after power-filled verse. I sat there in awe and wondered how in the world something so wonderful could even be possible. I thought to myself, "I am not good at memorizing scripture, but I want that ability in my life! How could I do that?" I really didn't know how to do it at the time but it became a deep-seated desire of my heart, a vision with seemingly unreachable goals in the beginning of this journey.

I looked up scriptures and found in John 14:12-26 (AMP) -- [12] I assure you *and* most solemnly say to you, anyone who believes in Me [as Savior] will also do the things that I do; and he will do even greater things than these [in extent and outreach], because I am going to the Father. [13] And I will do whatever you ask in My name [as My representative], this I will do, so that the Father may be glorified *and* celebrated in the Son. [14] If you ask Me anything in My name [as My representative], I will do it.[15] "If you [really] love Me, you will keep *and* obey My commandments.

The Role of the Spirit

[16] And I will ask the Father, and He will give you another Helper (Comforter, Advocate, Intercessor—Counselor, Strengthener, Standby), to be with you forever— [17] the Spirit of Truth, whom the world cannot receive [and take to its heart] because it does not see Him or know Him, *but* you know Him because He (the Holy Spirit) remains with you *continually* and will be in you.

[18] "I will not leave you as orphans [comfortless, bereaved, and helpless]; I will come [back] to you. [19] After a little while the world will no longer see Me, but you will see Me; because I live, you will live also. [20] On that day [when that time comes] you will know for yourselves that I am in My Father, and you *are* in Me, and I *am* in you. [21] The person who has My commandments and keeps them is the one who [really] loves Me; and whoever [really] loves Me will be loved by My Father, and I will love him and reveal Myself to him [I will make Myself real to him]." [22] Judas (not Iscariot) asked Him, "Lord, what has happened that You are going to reveal Yourself to us and not to the world?" [23] Jesus answered, "If anyone [really] loves Me, he will keep My word (teaching); and My Father will love him, and We will come to him and make Our dwelling place with him. [24] One who does not [really] love Me does not keep My words. And the word (teaching) which you hear is not Mine, but is the Father's who sent Me.

[25] "I have told you these things while I am still with you. [26] **But the Helper (Comforter, Advocate, Intercessor—Counselor, Strengthener, Standby), the Holy Spirit**, whom the Father will send in My name [in My place, to represent Me and act on My behalf], **He will teach you**

all things. **And He will help you remember everything that I have told you**.

That's it!!! I alone couldn't do it, but the Holy Spirit would help me do it!!! So, on the basis of this Word, I asked the Lord to help me memorize scripture so that I too could hide His Word in my heart and speak it forth when the need arose. He has sent many books into my paths over the years to help me do just that, but the very first thing I did was to sit down with my Bible and type up page after page of scriptures about specific topics that were important to me at that time. I entitled each page with subjects such as Healing, Peace and Safety, then looked in the concordance in the back of my Bible to find verses that pointed to those subjects. Years later, it is even easier with all the wonderful technology available to us at our fingertips online.

Each day I would speak these Words of God out loud, for He told us that "All of the Promises of God are YES and AMEN to the Glory of God **when we speak them**," and "there has not failed **one word** of all of His good Promises." Our words are a product of our thought life, whether that be controlled by our flesh which produces death, or by God's Spirit which is the key to living the abundant life that Jesus came to give us through the Blood Covenant His Father made with Him for our sakes. Our words are full of power, either to build up or to tear down, to plant or to dig up, to help or to hurt, to encourage or to discourage. God spoke the universe into existence by His Word, and we are His representatives (we "RE-present" Him to the people around us as Dutch Sheets so brilliantly stated in his book Intercessory Prayer).

As I mentioned earlier, there are wonderful books already written to help us carry out this vital ministry. Books such as Praying God's Word by Beth Moore, Prayers that Avail Much by Germaine Copeland, and The Power of a Praying Husband, The Power of a Praying Wife, The Power of a Praying Parent, etc. by Stormie Omartian. All of these are absolute treasures that have helped me along my life's path, to pray God's Will by praying His Word, which then becomes a natural part of our thinking, thus our speaking. Anyone **can** do it, and I am absolutely convinced that it is God's Will that everyone **would** do it!

So, as I was saying at the beginning of this chapter, is there anyone you know whose heart is icy and cold toward God; anyone who has a hard, impenetrable heart which seemingly cannot be opened up to the Love of Christ? God says to you and to me, "Is not My Word like as a fire, and like a hammer that breaks the rock in pieces?" Let the fire of His eternal Word melt that frigid heart. Speak forth His Word and let Him break that hard heart in pieces with the gentle but effective Hammer of God's Love to reveal a softly beating, tender heart toward our Creator. You be the vehicle through whom God works to transform a human life that is separated from Him by the words in which they presently believe. It is time to make and to be the difference!

THE FOOTBALL CAMERA

Several years ago, my dear sister-in-law Carol had encouraged me to journal each day. She had been journaling for years and had been extremely blessed in so doing, hearing regularly from the Lord. I knew in my heart that she was probably right and that I really should "just do it" but I was honestly just too lazy to begin the spiritual discipline which, I finally discovered, would open up such a stream of communication between the Lord and me that I had never experienced prior to that time. I must say that I am very sorry I missed so many God-given opportunities to hear His Voice and receive Holy Spirit-led direction due to the years of neglecting this powerful tool.

I believe with all of my heart that one of the reasons, and this is crucial, that journaling is so important is that when we DO hear God speak, we naturally tend to think, "Oh, I will NEVER forget this, it's SO awesome!!!" It reminds me of some great advice my dear friend Doreen gave me years ago when the Lord, after 9 years of marriage, finally gave my husband Randy and me the first of our two precious children. She told me "Becky, you need to write down all these special little things Beth (and later Grace) are doing. You think you'll always remember them, but you won't." Well, lo and behold, although I did write down a lot, I should have been more conscientious about it because things that I really KNEW I would never forget have slipped into the shadows of history without documentation. How foolish of me!!! Please learn from my mistake.

In Habakkuk 2:2-3 (AMP), God spoke clearly to His Prophet and to His people these important Words: [2] Then the LORD answered me and said, "Write the vision and engrave it plainly on [clay] tablets so that the one who reads it will run. [3] For the vision is yet for the appointed [future] time. It hurries toward the goal [of fulfillment]; it will not fail. Even though it delays, wait [patiently] for it, because it will certainly come; it will not delay."

You see, our loving and Omniscient Heavenly Father KNOWS that we are but dust and that we need the written word to help us in remembering the vital-for-our-very-life things He speaks to us, so that we will have the confidence to run with His words when He directs us to do so.

Soooo...one day I finally gave in to Carol's excellent advice and looked up a scripture in I Peter 5:6 (AMP) which goes "⁶Therefore humble yourselves under the mighty hand of God [set aside self-righteous pride], so that He may exalt you [to a place of honor in His service] at the appropriate time."

I wrote it down on a little pad of paper just as Carol had told me to do, sat there and thought about it, then asked God a question, not having a clue as to what to expect next. I said, "God, just what does this scripture really mean? I can't imagine that it means that if I humble myself before You that You will lift me up so that I will be better than others around me, right?" He promptly spoke to my heart and said, "You're right, it doesn't mean that at all! What I mean is that when you truly humble yourself before Me, THEN I will lift you up to a level from which you can see people, things and situations from MY Perspective. THEN you will know what the problem is and THEN you'll have My thoughts to know what to do about it." "Wow!" I thought. I had no idea! And thus the beginning of a whole new level of communication with the Lord.

So one Sunday afternoon awhile later, my husband Randy and I were sitting in our family room watching a professional football game together. You've got to know that I really love football and had watched hundreds of games throughout my lifetime. Suddenly there appeared on the television screen a camera angle I had never, ever seen before. It was as if the cameraman was lying down on his stomach in the back corner of the end zone while the two teams were out on the 20 yard line, ready for action. I stood up and said loudly, "Now why in the world would they do that?!!! I can't tell a thing about what's going on out there on the field!" Then slowly for surely, as my younger brother Chuck used to say when he was little, the camera began to rise up, up, up, higher and higher until you could see everything on the field very clearly. You could tell exactly who was open for a pass or where the defense opened up for a run, even though moments before you couldn't tell a thing about what would possibly work. The Lord graciously spoke to me and said, "My Child, THAT'S what I'm talking about! When you lay down your preconceived notions and presumed know-it-all-attitude about why somebody is the way they are or why something happened the way it did, THEN and ONLY then will I let you in on what I know about the problem and what needs to be done to resolve it!"

So do yourself a huge favor. Sit down with your Bible in your lap, toss out your old "self stuff", wait until God sends His Word down, just for your hearing, then write it down. It will change your life!!! Oh, and one more word of advice that I have learned from experience: Whatever He tells you, keep it to yourself until **HE** gives you the okay to run with it!!! This is HIS football game!

DAD AND THE WAVES

Way back in the winter of 1960, my family and I moved from snowy Bristol, Tennessee, two days after Christmas, to sunny Florida, where we had been coming to see relatives for years. My two brothers and sister and I couldn't believe we were actually going to be living in the land of coconut palms and sandy beaches. It was absolutely a dream come true.

I vividly recall our family driving to the beach in January and actually swimming in the ocean as people walking down the beach would look at us as if they couldn't believe the pale-skinned "nuts" they were seeing frolicking in the frigid waters. But before we became Florida "thin bloods", we saw no problem whatsoever in jumping headlong into the waves and loving every minute of it. What great memories of our first years here.

One of my favorites was of my dear Dad and me plowing through the waves and standing there letting them crash on us. My Dad would pick me up and put me on his shoulders so that I was not submerged each time a wave would pass around us. I just remember how extremely safe I felt, although poor Dad would be under water half the time, as I enjoyed my high place of protection with his arms wrapped snugly around my legs to keep me from falling from the impact of the waves.

It was years later that he showed us all a photo his pilot friend had taken as he had flown over the east coast of Florida, near where we had been playing at the beach. Right out in the waves, the same distance my Dad and I had walked out and stood to enjoy their crashing, there were sharks in the photo. What!!! Sharks!! I had no idea that these fierce, man-eating creatures had probably been swimming all around us as we stood there, safe and sound, so I had thought. I was amazed and aghast at this sight and couldn't take my eyes off of the picture. We could have been eaten alive and never seen again!!!

And then God showed me, from this picture I now had in my head, how He, our loving Heavenly Father, walks with us out into situations in which we are totally unaware of the dangers and pitfalls ahead; how He lovingly picks us up with His strong hands and wraps His big arms around our scrawny little legs to hold us up and out of evils and dangers of which we are totally unaware. I believe that we will perhaps never know until we reach those golden shores of Heaven all the many things Satan had planned for us which were thwarted by God's protective arms. Oh, praise God from Whom all blessings flow! Thank You, O Lord God Almighty, for your loving care of your precious children.

In Psalm 91 (AMP), one of my absolute favorite scripture passages, I want to share with you just a bite-sized portion of the picture of God's care of you and me as we believe His Word:

"He who dwells in the shelter of the Most High will remain secure *and* rest in the shadow of the Almighty [whose power no enemy can withstand]. ^{2} I will say of the LORD, 'He is my refuge and my fortress, My God, in whom I trust [with great confidence, and on whom I rely]!' ^{3} For He will save you from the trap of the fowler, and from the deadly pestilence. ^{4} He will cover you *and* completely protect you with His pinions (feathers), and under His wings you will find refuge; His faithfulness is a shield and a wall.

^{5} You will not be afraid of the terror of night, nor of the arrow that flies by day, ^{6} nor of the pestilence that stalks in darkness, nor of the destruction (sudden death) that lays waste at noon. ^{7} A thousand may fall at your side and ten thousand at your right hand, but danger will not come near you. ^{8} You will only [be a spectator as you] look on with your eyes and witness the [divine] repayment of the wicked [as you watch safely from the shelter of the Most High].

^{9} Because you have made the LORD, [who is] my refuge, even the Most High, your dwelling place, ^{10} No evil will befall you, nor will any plague come near your tent. ^{11} For He will command His angels in regard to you, to protect *and* defend *and* guard you in all your ways [of obedience and service].

[12] They will lift you up in their hands, so that you do not [even] strike your foot against a stone. [13] You will tread upon the lion and cobra; the young lion and the serpent you will trample underfoot.

[14] Because he set his love on Me, therefore I will save him; **I will set him [securely] on high, because he knows My name [he confidently trusts and relies on Me, knowing I will never abandon him, no, never].** [15] He will call upon Me, and I will answer him; I will be with him in trouble; I will rescue him and honor him. [16] "With a long life I will satisfy him and I will let him see My salvation."

And in Isaiah 43:1b-3a (TLB)-- "Do not be afraid, for I have ransomed you. I have called you by name; you are mine. [2] **When you go through deep waters, I will be with you.** When you go through rivers of difficulty, you will not drown. When you walk through the fire of oppression, you will not be burned up; the flames will not consume you. [3] **For I am the LORD, your God,** the Holy One of Israel, **your Savior."**

What an awesome Daddy He is to His beloved children! And what a blessed peace we have when we are resting, above the waves, in His everlasting Arms!

THE FORTRESS

Many years ago at the church Randy and I were attending at that time a touring group came to our fellowship and performed several dramatic skits for the congregation. They were truly excellent in their portrayal of the Truths they were passing on to all of us, and one skit in particular had a very profound effect on my heart and life. I would like to share it with you.

In this silent skit, there were four actors, two young ladies and two young men. The first young lady portrayed a seemingly lost, drug-addicted and hopeless person who met a young lady who had compassion for her, who ministered to her by counseling her, and who, when the first young lady's name came to her mind, would stop what she was doing and pray for her. The powerful fact here was that each time she stopped to pray, a young man dressed in white wielding an invisible sword would engage in battle with a young man dressed in black, also wielding an invisible sword. As long as the second young lady prayed, two things would occur. The first young lady would cease the thoughts and behavior she had been entertaining, and the young man in black would cower before the sword of the young man dressed in white.

But sadly, when the second young lady would stop praying, the first young lady would go right back to what she had been doing, and the young man dressed in black would gain ground in his attack on the young man in white. This cycle went on and on throughout the skit until finally, after the second young lady had consistently interceded for the first young lady many times, the young man in white soundly defeated the young man in black AND the first young lady humbly knelt down with the second young lady and prayed to receive Christ as her Lord and Savior. They joyously hugged and stood together with outreached arms in praise to God! Both of their lives were changed due to the impact of the second young lady's fervent and persistent intercession, and the resulting surrender of the first young lady's life to the Lord.

This dramatic presentation, as I stated above, so powerfully engrained itself in my thinking for years afterwards, so much so that I had a vision while in an intercessory prayer meeting one morning. It was a very similar scenario except that this time the first young lady was in a huge, impenetrable fortress surrounded by such thick darkness, full of hopelessness and despair. There were two huge demonic creatures standing guard outside the foreboding double wooden and metal doors with their spears in their hands. BUT… outside was the second young lady, out in the light of day, who, as she had done in the skit, would think of that first young lady and stop what she was doing to pray for her deliverance from the things in her life that held her in such tortuous bondage.

The awesome thing about this vision was that each time the second young lady would pray, although neither one of them could tell that there was any difference in the life of the first young lady who was hopelessly going around in circles, bumping into walls, getting nowhere it seemed to both of them, she was actually getting closer and closer to those huge imprisoning doors. And one day, in her darkness and unbeknownst to her, she stumbled right up to those enormous doors. The Lord spoke loudly and clearly to those huge demons who held her inside and said, "In Jesus' name, You open those doors and let her go free!!!!" Now it states in God's Word that even the demons must bow at the name of Jesus (Philippians 2:9-11 AMP), and that's exactly what they did!!! Those doors flew open and as they did, she came out, slowly at first, with her hand shielding her squinting eyes and her face contorted due to the unfamiliar brightness of the sun.

The young lady outside witnessed all that had just occurred, ran to her with open arms, and joyfully embraced the young lady who had been set free as a result of her prayers. They laughed and cried and rejoiced in her freedom as answered prayer was fulfilled before their very eyes. It was such an encouragement to me to never give up praying for someone, even when it appears to be a hopeless cause with no visible results for all of our efforts. Be encouraged by these words: "Let us not grow **weary** *or* become discouraged in doing good, for at the proper time we will reap, if we do not give in." Galatians 6:9 (AMP)

Years later, I was given a sequel to the first vision. Same fortress, same demon guards, same huge wooden and metal doors, but with two big differences. This time there was a crowd of many hopeless, despairing individuals inside the thick darkness of the fortress crying out as they continually bumped into each other while they aimlessly walked in circles and stumbled to the ground. This time, rather than one single intercessor there was a multitude of people outside the fortress who were willing to take the time to pray for them every time the Lord put them on their hearts, and many times in groups, asking God to save and deliver souls.

Same absence of recognition of any changes taking place, either by those who were trapped in their strongholds, or by those who were asking God to set them free. There was simultaneous hopelessness in their seemingly inescapable habits that pulled them mercilessly down to the pit, and expectant intercession in the lives of those who had themselves been set free by the Truth of the Word of God, no matter where their lifestyles had taken them in their past. Until….that glorious day when those demons once again heard that thundering Voice from Heaven…..but with a twist.

When God spoke this time, it was not for them to open the doors. When He spoke on this occasion, the entire fortress came crashing down to the ground allowing the prisoners to see the light of day as they had never seen it before. Once they had time to adjust their eyes to the light, they joyfully climbed over and out of the dust and the rubble, permitting the faithful ones who had spent countless hours in prayer to unite with these once imprisoned souls who were now free to enjoy the abundant life Jesus had promised, as the enemy of our souls had been defeated once again. Read here what Jesus said about this in John 10:10 (AMP) [10] "The thief comes only in order to steal and kill and destroy. I came that they may have *and* enjoy life, and have it in abundance [to the full, till it overflows]." Praise God!

Then, in February of 2014, a second sequel manifested. And this time it was the same fortress, the same demon guards, and the same doors, but the prisoner, it appeared, was Lady Liberty, the symbol of this great nation of ours here in America. This emblem which once stood tall for all that our founding fathers had fought and died for, the freedom of religion and worship according to His Word. This lady who upheld righteousness according to the Word of God Who sent His Word to heal us and to deliver us from all of our destructions (Psalm 107:20 NASB). Jehovah God, the One Who wants us to enjoy that awesome life of freedom from guilt and condemnation which comes when we are obedient to and trust in His Word and in His holy character. Character which is motivated by the most powerful force in existence, His unconditional Love for each and every one of us, no matter where we've been, what we've done or what has held us in bondage.

I have not seen the conclusion of this vision at this point in time. I believe that our merciful God has given us chance after chance after chance, as the Apostle John wrote in 1 John 1:9 (AMP): **"If we [freely] admit that we have sinned *and* confess our sins, He is faithful and just [true to His own nature and promises], and will forgive our sins and cleanse us *continually* from all unrighteousness [our wrongdoing, everything not in conformity with His will and purpose]."**

Read these life-giving, powerful words from 2 Chronicles 7:13-14----[13] *If* I shut up the heavens so that no rain falls, or if I command locusts to devour the land, or if I send pestilence *and* plague among My people, [14] and **My people, who are called by My Name, humble themselves, and pray and seek (crave, require as a necessity) My face and turn from their wicked ways, <u>then</u> I will hear [them] from heaven, and forgive their sin and <u>heal their land</u>.**

This Jesus, the Son of God Who was born of supernatural virgin birth, Who lived on this earth and was tempted just as we are yet without sin, Who did miracles for those who asked and for some who did not, Who was willing to suffer one of the most horrendous deaths ever experienced by man, was triumphantly raised by God's Spirit from the dead to give US new life in Him. He <u>will</u> forgive us of our sins and cleanse us from all our unrighteous ways.

Soak in this awesome Truth from Hebrews 4:12 (AMP)-- [12] "For the word of God is living and active *and* full of power [making it operative, energizing, and effective]. It is sharper than any two-edged sword, penetrating as far as the division of the soul and spirit [the completeness of a person], and of both joints and marrow [the deepest parts of our nature], exposing *and* judging the very thoughts and intentions of the heart." He KNOWS us inside and out! We can't hide from Him. Even still, in His Love and Mercy His arms are open wide, inviting us to enter into a relationship that is beyond our comprehension. I know. I've done it!!! He is day by day changing my life for the better!!! He will, my friend, do the same for you as well.

[34] Opening his mouth, Peter said: "I most certainly understand *now* that **_God is not one to show partiality_**," Acts 10:34 (NASB). It's true! No matter where you've been or what you've done, He loves you with an everlasting Love and wants you to be His Child.

My prayer is that we as individuals, that we as a nation, and that every nation on earth will have the eyes of our hearts opened to Truth, THE TRUTH, to step out of darkness into His marvelous light, and that we would be set free to live that abundant life both now and for all the ages to come.

THE WHOLE ARMOR OF GOD

For many, many years, due to the teaching of some wonderful servants of God on television, I have spoken and acted out the "putting on" of the whole armor of God over our entire family, and many more people for whom I pray, daily. I remember one of those teachers giving instructions something like this, "When you do not put on the whole armor of God, it's like going to your closet, choosing something to wear and expecting IT to jump off the rack and onto you." YOU **have** to take action. YOU **must** put it on!!! And YOU **cannot** afford to begin your day spiritually naked.

In Ephesians 6:10-18 God's Word states in the Amplified Bible:

[10] In conclusion, be strong in the Lord [be empowered through your union with Him]; draw your strength from Him [that strength which His boundless might provides]. [11] **Put on God's whole armor** [the armor of a heavily-armed soldier which God supplies], <u>that you may be able successfully to stand up against [all] the strategies *and* the deceits of the devil.</u>[12] For we are NOT wrestling with flesh and blood [contending only with physical opponents], but against the despotisms, against the powers, against [the master spirits who are] the world rulers of this present darkness, against the spirit forces of wickedness in the heavenly (supernatural)sphere. [13] **Therefore put on God's complete armor**, <u>that you may be able to resist *and* stand your ground on the evil day [of danger] (AND DOESN'T IT SEEM THAT THAT DAY IS HERE—NOW!), and, having done all [the crisis demands], to stand [firmly in your place].</u>[14] Stand therefore [hold your ground], having tightened the belt of TRUTH around your loins and having put on the breastplate of integrity *and* of moral rectitude *and* RIGHTEOUSNESS with God,[15] And having shod your feet in preparation [to face the enemy with the firm-footed stability, the promptness, and the readiness produced by the good news] of the GOSPEL of peace.[16] Lift up over all the [covering] shield of saving FAITH, upon which you can quench all the flaming missiles of the wicked [one].[17] And

take the helmet of SALVATION and the SWORD that the Spirit wields, which is the WORD OF GOD.[18] Pray at all times (on every occasion, in every season) in the Spirit, with all [manner of] prayer and entreaty. To that end keep alert and watch with strong purpose *and* perseverance, interceding in behalf of all the saints (God's consecrated people).

As I pondered each piece of that awesome armor which is listed for us in the above scriptures, I began to envision something so vitally important to our faith. I could see that each piece of the armor is actually Jesus Christ Himself! **We are to PUT ON JESUS**, and here's how I came to that conclusion:

It states in Ephesians 6 that we are to gird our loins (the very seat of our passions) with TRUTH. Jesus said in John 14:6 KJV, "I am the Way, the TRUTH, and the Life; no one comes to the Father but by Me." Jesus Christ is the fulfillment of every Word spoken by God through His servants the Prophets and by Jesus Himself, Who is God the Father in the Person of His Son made manifest in the flesh. God's Word says in John 1:14 (KJV)—"And THE WORD became flesh, and dwelt among us, and we beheld His Glory, Glory as of the only begotten from the Father, full of Grace and TRUTH." JESUS.

We are told to put on the breastplate of RIGHTEOUSNESS (the piece of the armor that protects our heart and our very breath). In 1 Corinthians 1:29-31 in the Amplified Bible it tells us this: "[29] So that no mortal man should [have pretense for glorying and] boast in the presence of God. [30] **But it is from Him that you have your life in Christ Jesus**, Whom God made Wisdom from God, [revealed to us a knowledge of the divine plan of salvation, manifesting itself as] **our RIGHTEOUSNESS** [thus making us upright and putting us in right standing with God], and our Consecration [making us pure and holy], and our Redemption [providing our ransom from eternal penalty for sin]. [31] So then, as it is written, Let him who boasts *and* proudly rejoices *and* glories, boast *and* proudly rejoice *and* glory in the Lord." JESUS.

As we prepare to meet the enemy (Satan and his demons who by an outrageous act of pride rebelled against the Word and Rule of God in Heaven, and were banished from ever permanently inhabiting that realm again) we are told to shod our feet with the preparation of the GOSPEL of Peace. The GOSPEL---the good news that Jesus Christ came into the world to save sinners, and that through the Blood Covenant which Creator God initiated through Jesus because of our great need for a Savior, we might have abundant life here on this earth and in the life hereafter. He did this even with all the wrong we have committed against God's Word which is the TRUTH, and made it possible for us to be completely forgiven by God. What a gift!!! What great LOVE!!! What GOOD NEWS!!! The GOSPEL!!! JESUS!

We have been graciously given the shield of FAITH to hold up in order to withstand all the fiery darts of the devil and his demons (the insidious thoughts He attempts to embed in our minds). Now God's Word tells us that "**FAITH comes by hearing and hearing by the Word of God concerning Jesus Christ**" in Romans 10:17. We learn in Romans 12:2-4 in the New International Version that we have all been given a measure of FAITH from God: "² Do not conform to the pattern of this world, but be transformed by the renewing of your mind (by meditating on and speaking forth the Word of God). Then you will be able to test and approve what God's will is—his good, pleasing and perfect will.³ For by the grace given me I say to every one of you: Do not think of yourself more highly than you ought, but rather think of yourself with sober judgment, in accordance with the FAITH God has distributed to each of you." Once again, JESUS!

I heard something so impactful years ago that I would like to share with you now. In the times of the Roman Empire, as the battalions of very well trained and rugged soldiers marched from conquest to conquest, they would proceed in very tight formations. The soldiers in the front held up their shields to the front. The soldiers on the sides held up their shields to the sides. The soldiers in the rear held up their shields to protect them from behind. And the soldiers in the middle of the formation held up their shields above them all, thus the maximum protection for each soldier and each group as a whole. What an awesome picture we should mimic as the Body of Christ, protecting not only ourselves but all for whom Christ died, and with whom we walk on a daily basis.

Next, we are to put on the Helmet of SALVATION which comes only through the name of Jesus according to Acts 4:8-12 in the Amplified,

"8 Then Peter, [because he was] filled with [and controlled by] the Holy Spirit, said to them, 'Rulers of the people and members of the council (the Sanhedrin), 9 If we are being put on trial [here] today *and* examined concerning a good deed done to benefit a feeble (helpless) cripple, by what means this man has been restored to health,10 Let it be known *and* understood by all of you, and by the whole house of Israel, that **in the name and through the power *and* authority of Jesus Christ of Nazareth**, Whom you crucified, [but] Whom God raised from the dead, **in Him *and* by means of Him this man is standing here before you well *and* sound in body**.11 **This Jesus** is the Stone which was despised *and* rejected by you, the builders, but which has become the Head of the corner [the Cornerstone].12-**And there is SALVATION in *and* through no one else, for there is no other name under heaven given among men by *and* in which we must be saved**.'" It's JESUS!! Our SALVATION!!!

And finally, in the sequence of putting on all the parts of God's armor, comes one of my absolute favorites: **the SWORD of the Spirit**, the offensive weapon, which is **the WORD OF GOD**. Take a look at what John 1:1-6 speaks to us in the Amplified Bible:

"1 In the beginning [before all time] was **THE WORD (Christ),** and **THE WORD was with God**, and **THE WORD was God Himself**. 2 He was present originally with God. 3 All things were made *and* came into existence through Him; and without Him was not even one thing made that has come into being. 4 In Him was Life, and the Life was the Light of men."

Hebrews 4:12 in the Amplified powerfully explains this Truth to us:

"12 **For THE WORD that God speaks is alive and full of power [making it active, operative, energizing, and effective]; it is sharper than any two-edged sword**, penetrating to the dividing line of the breath of life (soul) and [the immortal] spirit, and of joints and marrow [of the deepest parts of our nature], exposing *and* sifting *and* analyzing *and* judging the very thoughts and purposes of the heart." ALWAYS JESUS!!!

Now remember from God's Word in Ephesians 6, we ARE NOT fighting against flesh and blood, or against people. We ARE, or need to be, waging a war against Satan and all his demons, who most definitely do USE people to try to wreak havoc in our lives, but who are themselves evil spirit beings and as such MUST be fought with spiritual weapons—God's Word, Praise, Obedience, Worship. We MUST protect ourselves, and those we love, with spiritual armor. And God says to us in 2 Peter 1:2-4 In the Amplified: "² <u>May Grace</u> (God's favor) <u>and Peace</u> (which is perfect well-being, all necessary good, all spiritual prosperity, and freedom from fears and agitating passions and moral conflicts<u>) be multiplied to you in</u> [the full, personal, precise, and correct] <u>knowledge of God and of</u> **Jesus our Lord**.

³ **For His divine power has bestowed upon us ALL things that [are requisite and suited] to life and godliness, through the [full, personal] knowledge of Him Who called us by** *and* **to His own glory and excellence (virtue).**⁴ By means of these He has bestowed on us **His precious and exceedingly great promises** (His WORD!), so that **through them** (His WORD) you may escape [by flight] from the moral decay (rottenness and corruption) that is in the world because of covetousness (lust and greed), and become sharers (partakers) of the divine nature." This is absolutely NOTHING we deserve, but through Grace He has freely bestowed this gift upon us, through the Blood Covenant!

So I encourage you, brothers and sisters, even before you get out of bed in the morning, arm yourself, your family, your friends, your employees, your co-workers, your schoolmates, all those about whom you care, with the full armor of God…each and every day of your life. Act it out as you speak it forth. Envision each part of the armor as you put it on and realize that you are clothing yourselves and those for whom you are praying with Jesus Christ Himself, the One Who has all power in Heaven and earth. The One Who has chosen to be in Blood Covenant with you and with all of your descendants who come after you, and with those who believe the good news of the Gospel because of your prayers of faith. What a legacy we can leave behind! What a **divine inheritance** to pass down to the generations ahead of us!!! It's ours for the taking!!! LET'S DO IT!!!

LOST AND FOUND

Several years ago, after I had been working at my husband's law office as the file clerk and receptionist initially, then as the bookkeeper and office manager later, our legal assistant was in great need of a certain type of document in dealing with one of our client's cases. She searched high and low throughout the office. She called other legal assistants she knew to ask them if they had ever heard of the document or knew where she could find it, and all to no avail. Extremely frustrated as you might imagine, and at a dead end to help our client, she and I decided to pray about the matter and asked God to reveal the document's whereabouts to us. In situations like this in which I have exhausted all resources to find something, I always love to go to the scriptures in Matthew 7: 7-8 (AMP) which are the words of Jesus: [7] "Ask *and* keep on asking and it will be given to you; seek *and* keep on seeking and you will find; knock *and* keep on knocking and the door will be opened to you. [8] For everyone who keeps on asking receives, and he who keeps on seeking finds, and to him who keeps on knocking, it will be opened."

These words have never failed me. It may take a little longer than I'm comfortable with but I have ALWAYS, so far, found every single thing I've ever lost and for which I've prayed God's Word.

Now when I first came to work at the office, years before this need arose, I had done a lot of reorganizing, and one of the things I had done in those early days was to accurately re-alphabetize all the file cards on which each of our client's names and pertinent contact information had been typed and placed into a file box when their case was first opened.

One night as I lay sleeping I had a dream and actually remembered my dream which was quite unusual for me, so this one really stuck with and puzzled me greatly. I saw, as if on a huge brilliantly lit neon sign, a person's name flashing. The name seemed vaguely familiar but I had no idea as to why I would have such a strange dream or why his name would be in it. I just tucked that one away and pretty much forgot about it, thinking it to be one of those unexplainable things in life, possibly due to what I had eaten that evening before going to bed.

After some time had passed, my husband came into the office from his court hearings one afternoon. Our legal assistant was relating to him her dilemma about the mysterious document. He, too, could not recall where she might find the document. Suddenly, as I overheard their conversation from my office, the thought occurred to me (and now we know why and from whence it came) to ask them if they had ever heard of the person's name I had seen flashing on the billboard of my dream. Upon my saying that name, both Randy and our assistant immediately recognized it as a client from years past, so I said to the assistant, "Let's find his file and see if there's anything unusual about it". So, after searching through the boxes of long ago closed files and locating his, she opened it up and there, right on top of all his paperwork, was THE document for which she had so fervently searched and for which we had prayed God's Word in faith to find.

What a loving and kind God we serve! He cares!!!

Matthew 6:8 (Good News Translation)-- [8] "Do not be like them. Your Father already knows what you need before you ask him." AMEN!!!

BATHROOM TERROR

One night many years ago, I had a dream. No, actually it was a nightmare!!! As I had mentioned previously, I usually don't remember my dreams at all, but this one was a biggie and it woke me up in a state of terror, as if it had actually happened. You know, the kind from which you wake up frantically gasping and sweating from fear.

The setting was a tall office building in a big city. It was nighttime, nobody around. I went into the ladies' restroom and into a stall and shut the door. The door to the ladies' room then opened. I sensed a foreboding presence in the room, and suddenly, there were men's boots showing under the door of my stall. Fear absolutely gripped me. I'm sure many of you have experienced a time in which you were dreaming and tried to scream but almost nothing but a tiny squeak would come out of your mouth. Well, that was me. I tried and tried to yell for help as the perpetrator violently and relentlessly attempted to remove the door of the stall in order to reach me to obviously do me great harm. It was absolutely horrific! When I awoke and after I calmed down, I thought, "Why in the world would I have a dream like that? What was that about?" It was SO scary and disturbing.

This dream puzzled me for years, with no answer forthcoming, until one night a sequel occurred. Same building, same bathroom, same stall, BUT, with a huge difference! This time, as the man entered the room and began beating on and trying to remove the stall door, I took action with a twist. I spoke calmly and with the authority we have been given as children of the Most High God. I told him, "In the name of Jesus, I command you to leave this place NOW! I am protected by the Blood of Jesus Christ, and covered with the whole Armor of God Almighty (you see how important that chapter was now)!!! You have NO power over me, for God has given His Angels charge over me to guard me in ALL my ways!!! LEAVE... NOW!!!"............................AND HE DID!!! AWESOME!!!

I thought, "Okay, so that's what that was about. God was showing me the incredible difference between acting in the flesh in order to battle the demonic realm and acting in the Spirit with His authority and His Peace." I had not yelled or done anything in the physical realm, other than speak. I had done spiritual warfare and therefore had reaped the victory. Psalm 91, as we already discussed in "Dad and the Waves", is such a crucial chapter in our lives, yet how many of us are even aware of it, much less have hidden it in our hearts so that we're ready in a moment's notice for what may come?

Jeremiah 20:11 in the New American Standard Version says this to us: "**But the LORD is with me like a dread champion**; Therefore **my persecutors will stumble** and **not** **prevail**. **They will be utterly ashamed**, because **they have failed** with an everlasting disgrace that will not be forgotten".

Now let me say that just saying the Name of Jesus is not like speaking some magic words then the thing we want to have happen just happens. God's Word says that we are Ambassadors for Christ (2 Corinthians 5:20). This implies relationship, a mutual, close and trusting relationship wrought over time and with much contact and dialogue.

That's God's heart for us…a close, loving relationship built on prayer and study of His Love Letter to us, the Bible. He wants us to know Him as Father with all the caring that a good Daddy pours out on His children whom He loves. Then, as we experience life's good times and its trials, we come to really KNOW the Power and Authority of His Word, and are able to walk in that authority as we meet those challenges head-on. Read Luke 10:19 (AMP)-- [19] Listen carefully: I have given you authority (that you now possess) to tread on serpents and scorpions (demons), and the ability to exercise authority over all the power of the enemy (Satan); and nothing will (in any way) harm you.

I will never forget the awesome Truth God revealed to me in that two-part dream from a bathroom stall. Thank You, Lord, for great sequels!!!

THE VERTICAL CONVEYOR BELT

Many years ago, my husband and I were in church enjoying the singing when suddenly I had a vision of what I could only describe as a "vertical conveyor belt."

At the top of the conveyor belt, God in Heaven was sending down to each one of us His eternal Word, all the Promises He has spoken which cover every issue and problem in our lives. His Word, the very "dunamis", dynamite Power by which He spoke Creation into existence, can change all the seemingly unchangeable people and things in our lives that need changing, including ourselves in all our human frailty. That Sword of the Spirit that is alive and sharper than any two-edged sword, able to divide our soul and spirit, and to discern the very thoughts and intentions of our hearts. That divine Power source in which there has not failed ONE WORD of all His good Promises, for <u>all</u> of the Promises of God are Yes and Amen to His Glory, WHEN WE SPEAK THEM!!! For God's Word is TRUTH, Truth that transcends all of the "truth" of this world with all of its fleshly desires. Truth that sets the captives free, free from drug and alcohol addiction, sexual sin, every sin of the mind and heart. Truth that heals the broken-hearted and binds up their wounds.

His Word is one of the Power Tools He uses to do His eternal work here on earth, to hammer off hardened crud that's been there for years, even decades; to sand down sharp and jagged edges that cause pain to us and to others; to wash away with the Water of the Word (Ephesians 5:26) all the "dirt" that clogs up our spiritual arteries and keeps that life-giving Blood from flowing smoothly through our beings. God's eternal Word…It never changes in intent or in effect, which is to show us how very much He loves us and that He has and will fulfill an incredible Plan for each one of our lives when we surrender to His perfect will.

As God's Word came down to each one of us on this divine conveyor belt, God waited to see what we would do with It. Would we ignore It completely, never opening the Love Letter He has sent to each one of us revealing His Goodness and Mercy to those who choose to believe Him? Would we take a quick glance at the Bible, using it more as a coffee table decoration, but never taking the time to study and find the treasures hidden therein, or would we be diligent to read It, to memorize It so that It becomes a vital part of our very beings? God is such a Gentleman and will not violate our wills, so He patiently waits for us to make the choice that will affect not only us, but generations to come.

Then I saw people here on earth, those who chose to take God at His Word, to believe the One who sent His Son, The Word manifested in the flesh, and to trust in the authority and Power of that Word. They were speaking forth His Word in faith, faith that He would do what He said He would do, no matter how long it takes nor how hard the road ahead until the fruition of that Word comes to pass. They chose to speak that Word back up into the Heavenlies as a sweet smelling incense, a sacrifice of praise, and it filled the very nostrils of God. And He, as a loving Heavenly Father, was pleased.

Imagine this scenario, if you will. If you are a parent, or can just think like a parent, imagine your telling your child that if they will do _____(fill in the blank), then you will do_____(fill in the blank) as a result, because you love them and want to bless them for their trust and obedience. And then they actually remember what you said, believe you….and do it!!! And if you're still standing up, then you do what you said you would do because they did what you asked them to do!!! Wow!!! Does that thrill the heart of any Mom or Dad or what?!!! Well, multiply that joy a few trillion times, when we listen and believe what God speaks to us through His Word, and do what He asks us to do!!!.

Take this word to heart (Matthew 22:37-40 AMP) [36] "Teacher, which is the greatest commandment in the Law?" [37] And Jesus replied to him, 'You SHALL LOVE THE LORD YOUR GOD WITH ALL YOUR HEART, AND WITH ALL YOUR SOUL, AND WITH ALL YOUR MIND.' [38] This is the first and greatest commandment. [39] The second is like it, 'You SHALL LOVE YOUR NEIGHBOR

AS YOURSELF [that is, unselfishly seek the best or higher good for others].' [40] The whole Law and the [writings of the] Prophets depend on these two commandments."

So, God, Who is SO pleased with His kids who take Him up on His Word, sends His Word back down in Power on that Heavenly conveyor belt to do what He intended it to do…and that Power changes lives, for generations to come!!!! For He said in Isaiah 55:11 (NASB) "So will My word be which goes forth from My mouth; It will NOT return to Me empty, without accomplishing what I desire, and without succeeding *in the matter* for which I sent it", for "He sent His Word and and healed them and delivered them from their destructions!" (Psalm 107:20 KJV) Why? Very simply because "[16] God so loved the world, that he gave his only begotten Son (JESUS), that whosoever believeth in him should not perish, but have everlasting life. [17] For God sent not his Son into the world to condemn the world; but that the world through him might be saved." John 3:16 (KJV)

Take this in from I Peter 1:3-4 (AMP) [3] For His divine power has bestowed on us [absolutely] everything necessary for [a dynamic spiritual] life and godliness, through true *and* personal knowledge of Him who called us by His own glory and excellence. [4] For by these He has bestowed on us His precious and magnificent promises [of inexpressible value], **so that by them you may escape from the immoral freedom that is in the world because of disreputable desire, and become sharers of the divine nature.**

What an awesome Dad our Heavenly Father is to us!!! Believe Him today! You will never be sorry you did.

PRAISE HIM IN THE STORMS

One of the things that I believe is essential in the process of learning and growing is to, by faith, praise God in the storms of life, whether the storms are just little dust eddies that have the capability to frazzle our nerves on any given day, or are a category 5 hurricane that over time, or suddenly, erupts in our lives and can potentially damage our home and health. Now, depending on our response, one of these unexpected events can change our lives and the lives of those around us for years to come. When I think about this sure thing in life, these storms that we will all experience at one time or another, I see a picture in my mind from the movie, "The Perfect Storm," and envision myself or someone I know who is going through a tough time as the one floating on the tempest of life, one tiny almost undetectable dot surrounded by thousands of miles of monstrous waves with seemingly no hope of rescue. I would like to share with you some scriptures I have held onto as an anchor for my soul in some of the biggest storms of my life, so grab onto your life jackets!

Psalm 89:5-9, 14-18 (Message Bible)--God! Let the cosmos praise your wonderful ways, the choir of holy angels sing anthems to your faithful ways! Search high and low, scan skies and land, you'll find nothing and no one quite like God. The holy angels are in awe before him; he looms immense and august over everyone around him. God-of-the-Angel-Armies, who is like you, powerful and faithful from every angle? **You put the arrogant ocean in its place and calm its waves when they turn unruly**. The Right and Justice are the roots of your rule; Love and Truth are its fruits. **Blessed are the people who know the passwords of praise, who shout on parade in the bright presence of God. Delighted, they dance all day long; they know who You are, what You do—they can't keep it quiet! Your vibrant beauty has gotten inside us— you've been so good to us!**

We're walking on air! All we are and have we owe to You God, Holy God of Israel, our King!

Now be on the alert! A storm is brewing! Psalm 3:1-8 (Message)--¹⁻² GOD! Look! Enemies past counting! Enemies sprouting like mushrooms, mobs of them all around me, roaring their mockery: "Hah! No help for *him or her* from God!" ³⁻⁴ **But you, GOD, shield me on all sides; You ground my feet, you lift my head high; with all my might I shout up to GOD, His answers thunder from the holy mountain.** ⁵⁻⁶ **I stretch myself out. I sleep. Then I'm up again—rested, tall and steady, Fearless before the enemy mobs coming at me from all sides.** ⁷ Up, GOD! My God, help me! Slap their faces, First this cheek, then the other, Your fist hard in their teeth! ⁸ **Real help comes from GOD. Your blessing clothes your people!**

Always remember that the reason we can praise Him is because of His steadfast love for us.

Psalm 5:7-11 (Living Bible)-- ⁷ **But as for me, I will come into your Temple protected by your mercy and your love**; I will worship you with deepest awe. ⁸ Lord, lead me as you promised me you would; otherwise my enemies will conquer me. Tell me clearly what to do, which way to turn. ⁹ For they cannot speak one truthful word. Their hearts are filled to the brim with wickedness. Their suggestions are full of the stench of sin and death. Their tongues are filled with flatteries to gain their wicked ends. ¹⁰ O God, hold them responsible. Catch them in their own traps; let them fall beneath the weight of their own transgressions, for they rebel against you. ¹¹ **But make everyone rejoice who puts his trust in you. Keep them shouting for joy because you are defending them. Fill all who love you with your happiness.**

Our life of praise will be evident to everyone around us.

Psalm 9:1-2; 9-14 (Message)-- ¹⁻² **I'm thanking you, GOD, from a full heart**, I'm writing the book on your wonders. **I'm whistling, laughing, and jumping for joy; I'm singing your song, High God.** ⁹⁻¹⁰ GOD's a safe-house for the battered, a sanctuary during bad times. The moment you arrive, you relax; you're never sorry you knocked. ¹¹⁻¹² **Sing your songs** to Zion-dwelling G<small>OD</small>; tell his stories to everyone you meet: How he tracks down killers yet keeps his eye on us, registers every whimper and moan. [13-14] Be kind to me, G<small>OD</small>; I've been kicked around long enough. Once you've pulled me back from the gates of death, **I'll write the book on Hallelujahs**; on the corner of Main and First I'll hold a street meeting; **I'll be the song leader; we'll fill the air with salvation songs**.

Psalm 13:3-6 (Message)--[3-4] Take a good look at me, G<small>OD</small>, my God; I want to look life in the eye, so no enemy can get the best of me or laugh when I fall on my face. [5-6] I've thrown myself headlong into your arms-- **I'm celebrating your rescue. I'm singing at the top of my lungs, I'm so full of answered prayers.**

Psalm 16:1-11 (Message)—[1-2] Keep me safe, O God, I've run for dear life to you. I say to G<small>OD</small>, "Be my Lord!" Without you, nothing makes sense. [3] And these God-chosen lives all around—what splendid friends they make! [4] Don't just go shopping for a god. Gods are not for sale. I swear I'll never treat god-names like brand-names. [5-6] **My choice is you, G<small>OD</small>, first and only. And now I find I'm *your* choice! You set me up with a house and yard. And then you made me your heir**!

Now THAT'S something to praise God about…we are His heirs according to the Promise!!!

[7-8] **The wise counsel G<small>OD</small> gives when I'm awake is confirmed by my sleeping heart. Day and night I'll stick with G<small>OD</small>; I've got a good thing going and I'm not letting go.** [9-10] **I'm happy from the inside out, and from the outside in, I'm firmly formed. You canceled my ticket to hell—that's not my destination!** [11] **Now you've got my feet on the life path, all radiant from the shining of your face. Ever since you took my hand, I'm on the right way.**

The following Psalm was especially comforting and empowering to me during a very dark time in my life.

Psalm 18:1-6, 16-40a; 46-50 (NASB)-- **"I love You, O L<small>ORD</small>, my strength." [2] The L<small>ORD</small> is my rock and my fortress and my deliverer,**

My God, my rock, in whom I take refuge; My shield and the horn of my salvation, my stronghold. ³ **I call upon the** Lord, **who is worthy to be praised, and I am saved from my enemies**. ⁴ The cords of death encompassed me, and the torrents of ungodliness terrified me. ⁵ The cords of Sheol surrounded me; the snares of death confronted me. ⁶ In my distress I called upon the Lord, and cried to my God for help; **He heard my voice out of His temple, and my cry for help before Him came into His ears.**

¹⁶ **He sent from on high, He took me; He drew me out of many waters.** ¹⁷ **He delivered me from my strong enemy, and from those who hated me, for they were too mighty for me.** ¹⁸ **They confronted me in the day of my calamity, but the** Lord **was my stay.** ¹⁹ **He brought me forth also into a broad place; He rescued me, because He delighted in me.**

Now look at this!!!:

²⁰ **The** Lord **has rewarded me according to my <u>righteousness</u>** (due to our relationship with Jesus); according to the cleanness of my hands He has recompensed me. ²¹ For I have kept the ways of the Lord, and have not wickedly departed from my God. ²² For all His ordinances were before me, and I did not put away His statutes from me. ²³ I was also blameless with Him, and I kept myself from my iniquity. ²⁴ Therefore the Lord has recompensed me according to my righteousness, according to the cleanness of my hands in His eyes.

²⁵ With the kind You show Yourself kind; with the blameless You show Yourself blameless; ²⁶ with the pure You show Yourself pure, and with the crooked You show Yourself astute. ²⁷ For You save an afflicted people, but haughty eyes You abase. ²⁸ **For You light my lamp; The** Lord **my God illumines my darkness.** ²⁹ **For by You I can run upon a troop; and by my God I can leap over a wall.**

Look! Here's that spiritual warfare and the whole armor of God again!!!

³⁰ **As for God, His way is blameless; The word of the** Lord **is tried; He is a shield to all who take refuge in Him.** ³¹ **For who is God, but the** Lord**? and who is a rock, except our God,** ³² **The God Who girds me**

with strength and makes my way blameless? ³³He makes my feet like hinds' *feet*, and sets me upon my high places. ³⁴He trains my hands for battle, So that my arms can bend a bow of bronze. ³⁵You have also given me the shield of Your salvation, and Your right hand upholds me; and Your gentleness makes me great. ³⁶You enlarge my steps under me, and my feet have not slipped.

³⁷ I pursued my enemies and overtook them, and I did not turn back until they were consumed. ³⁸ I shattered them, so that they were not able to rise; they fell under my feet. ³⁹ For You have girded me with strength for battle; You have subdued under me those who rose up against me. ⁴⁰ You have also made my enemies turn their backs to me.

⁴⁶ **The LORD lives, and blessed be my rock; and exalted be the God of my salvation,** ⁴⁷ The God who executes vengeance for me, and subdues peoples under me. ⁴⁸ **He delivers me from my enemies; surely You lift me above those who rise up against me; You rescue me from the violent man. ⁴⁹ Therefore I will give thanks to You among the nations, O LORD, and I will sing praises to Your name.** ⁵⁰ He gives great deliverance to His king, and shows lovingkindness to His anointed, to David and his descendants forever.

Now I need to tell you that that last one was a scripture that God used to minister powerfully to me, not once but twice. Once after 31 hours of labor with 2 solid hours of pushing with all my might for the delivery of our first precious child, and secondly when I went through 8 months of very serious cancer treatment when she was 9 years old and our youngest was 6. But this next one God used so specifically when we were waiting for that first baby for 7 long years, and then daily as He gradually expounded the whole chapter's meaning to me. It's become such an important part of my life.

Psalm 113:1-9 (NASB)-- **Praise the LORD! Praise, O servants of the LORD, Praise the name of the LORD. ²Blessed be the name of the LORD from this time forth and forever. ³From the rising of the sun to its setting, the name of the LORD is to be praised. ⁴The LORD is high above all nations; His glory is above the heavens.** ⁵Who is like the LORD our God, Who is enthroned on high, ⁶Who humbles Himself to behold *The* *things that are* in heaven and in the earth? ⁷ He raises the poor from the dust and lifts the needy from the ash heap, ⁸ to make *them* sit with princes, with the princes of His people. ⁹ **He makes the barren woman abide in the house *as* a joyful mother of children. Praise the LORD!**

And one last word of encouragement, straight from God's Word:

Psalm 116: 1-19 (Living Bible)--**I love the Lord because he hears my prayers and answers them. ²Because he bends down and listens, I will pray as long as I breathe**! ³ Death stared me in the face—I was frightened and sad. ⁴ Then I cried, "Lord, save me!" ⁵ **How kind he is! How good he is! So merciful, this God of ours**! ⁶ The Lord protects the simple and the childlike; I was facing death, and then he saved me. ⁷ **Now I can relax. For the Lord has done this wonderful miracle for me. ⁸ He has saved me from death, my eyes from tears, my feet from stumbling. ⁹ I shall live! Yes, in his presence—here on earth!**

¹⁰⁻¹¹ In my discouragement I thought, "They are lying when they say I will recover." ¹² **But now what can I offer Jehovah for all he has done for me?** ¹³ **I will bring him an offering** of wine **and praise his name for saving me**. ¹⁴ I will publicly bring him the sacrifice I vowed I would. ¹⁵ His loved ones are very precious to him, and he does not lightly let them die. ¹⁶ **O Lord, you have freed me from my bonds, and I will serve you forever. ¹⁷ I will worship you and offer you a sacrifice of thanksgiving.** ¹⁸⁻¹⁹ Here in the courts of the Temple in Jerusalem, before all the people, I will pay everything I vowed to the Lord. **Praise the Lord!**

And just one more that I love in the Message Bible—Psalm 4:6-8--⁶⁻⁷ Why is everyone hungry for *more*? "More, more," they say. "More, more." **I have God's more-than-enough, more joy in one ordinary day ⁷⁻⁸ than they get in all their shopping sprees. At day's end I'm ready for sound sleep, for you, GOD, have put my life back together.**

God's unchangeable Word is in the lifelong process of coming to pass in my life. Oh yes, there have been many times that I have chosen not to praise Him in the midst of my storms, I can assure you of that. For me there was no peace in that…..until I remembered what He had spoken to me, to all of us… to praise Him even when it seems foolish. Praise Him when all that is around us cries out for us to fear, to even doubt His existence much less His Goodness. BUT when we choose, when we make that life-changing decision to trust Him, to obey Him, to praise Him as we float helplessly in the trough of the 60 foot monstrous waves that are ready to crash down upon us to take us down for the last time, He has and will always come through to pull us out of the tempest which seeks to destroy our hope and our very lives. Choose life, choose praise, and see just what God can and WILL do….for **you**.

THE COMFORT CHUTE

What in the world, you might ask, is a comfort chute??? Well, let me tell you, this was a vision the Lord gave me more than 30 years ago during a very dark time in my life. You see, my dear husband Randy and I had been trusting and believing that the Lord would bless us with a child, a child that I longed to hold, to love, and to care for. Seven years of my tears as I watched couple after couple, stranger after stranger with the woman's poochy tummy giving evidence that God had blessed them with the promise of a child. NOBODY knows how hard it is to go month after fruitless month, year after childless year, with no sign that anything is going to be different in this department.... unless you've been there yourself, and I know that many of you have!

Randy and I attended a church during that time in our lives in which it seemed like every couple either had a child, or children, or were pregnant. There was one couple that had EIGHT children in nine years. REALLY?!!! All I wanted was just one little baby, just one, Lord!!! The pain I experienced would be unbearable, over and over and over again!!! And the comments people would make at times were simply unbelievable. There was one person who would say things to me like, "When are you gonna give Randy a kid?" or "Randy needs a boy!" Back to the foot of my bed with tears of agony pouring out of my eyes, and one more opportunity to forgive.

One day I was in the grocery store minding my own business when this total stranger, a man, walked right up to me and said, "Why don't you have a baby? You should have a baby!" I was absolutely dumb-founded!!! Where did this guy come from, anyway? Straight from you know where, as far as I was concerned at that time.

Well, one of the things I did as an act of faith was to babysit, free of charge, for any of the families with children in our church......sort of "on the job training" for the child we believed would one day come into our lives. The one family who had the eight children provided a constant flow of "wannabemommy" practice for me each time they had another baby. We always chose to have the darling twin boys stay with us until the "new" parents had time to settle in with the latest arrival. I have to say, it was truly a blessing to be able to not only help these families, but to learn the ins and outs of parenting, and to have little ones to love while we waited on ours to get there.

Another thing I felt led to do, and as I had mentioned earlier, was to type page after page of scriptures on all the subjects that concerned me, which definitely included verses about childbearing. I poured over these scriptures every day, feeding my spirit with the Truths and Promises of God's Word, building my faith that the long-awaited Promise would come to pass in God's perfect timing for Randy and me. I later learned, as I mentioned previously, that there are awesome books out there that provide the same blessing, all typed up and ready to absorb. And so began my love for hiding God's Word in my heart, and therefore knowing how to pray God's Word for others.

The last thing I did was to prepare, in faith, a nursery for our little one who was to come. I had heard that the color yellow is a great stimulator for the brains of babies, so up went the yellow on those nursery walls. I lovingly and excitedly sewed the bed sheets and bumper pad covers and dust ruffle for the crib (which our dear friends Ed and Linda had contributed, along with the matching changing table) out of blue and white gingham checks, and prepared framed verses to place around the room. Another friend held one of those parties as part of her new job in selling educational materials for children, and I purchased a foldable alphabet teaching aid decorated with brightly colored pictures of apples and bananas and cats and all the rest to teach our new baby the alphabet when he or she arrived. But.......he or she did not arrive. Oh, the buckets of tears I cried every month when I was alone in our home. "Dear God, why? Why can't we have a baby like all of these other blessed couples??? Have we done something wrong to make You mad at us, to keep us from having a little one??? Pleeeeeeease help us,

O God!!! Please, I beg you!!! Give us a baby!!!!" Was He even hearing me??? It sure didn't seem so.

One week during this time, our church had a week-long nightly revival with authors Frank and Ida Mae Hammond as the guest speakers. During the altar call, I was so overcome with emotion that I didn't think I could make it through the rest of the service. I was emotionally and physically drained by the sheer grief that I carried as a result of our childlessness. I poured out my heart to the Lord, and waited to hear what He might say in return.

Suddenly, with my tear-stained eyes closed, I saw what appeared to be a huge chute, or a slide, coming down out of heaven and ending at my heart. There was a package at the top of the chute which was surrounded in a cloudy haze. Suddenly, a hand reached down from the haze and pushed the package off the top of the chute, sending it sliding down, down, down….right toward my breaking heart. Fear gripped me as I thought, "My heart is so full of pain, I couldn't stand to have this thing hit me right where I already hurt so much." But just as the package neared my tender, vulnerable heart, that same gentle hand reached down and stopped it right before impact. I winced but then realized that it was not going to hurt me, but that what was inside was the comfort of God, a comfort I so desperately needed right then, right there in that moment. Oh, the relief, the joy I felt, the miracle of God's healing hand upon me, the hope that exploded in my heart confirming what we had believed for so long.

The Lord spoke to my heart awhile after this occurrence telling me that we would have a baby, but He relayed the news in a very unusual way. My mother-in-law said that she had been vacuuming her floors in her home when suddenly she heard the Lord say, "Randy and Becky will have a baby in November." I was so thrilled when she relayed this to us.….. it was beyond words!!!

Now don't think it was all over at that point because it surely was not. This was February and that, as you may calculate, is only nine months away from November, and I was not pregnant. "What's going on, God?" I asked.

Randy's brother and our sister-in-law called to ask if we could keep their son, their second child, while they went on a trip, and of course we were more than happy to do so. When they brought him to our home, she told me that they were pregnant with their 3rd child, and that they were due in November. In November…. even as I type these words, my heart feels that twinge of pain I felt when I heard her speak those words more than 30 years ago. Oh God, I thought that Word was for us, but now I find out it's for someone else in the family. I am so happy for them, but Oh God, help me to endure. Help me to hang on to my faith in Your Word. Don't let me be discouraged once again, I prayed.

A dear friend of mine, at just the perfect time in this whole process of developing my faith, told me that she had had **a dream**. She saw her child who was not yet born, nor was she pregnant at the time, playing with my child, and that it was more real in her spirit than anything she had ever experienced. Well, I knew Punkin (don't you love that name?!) heard from The Lord because she spent so much time in prayer for others and in God's Word, meditating on His Promises. So, hope was restored in the nick of time, once again.

Time went on. One day I was cleaning our kitchen with Christian radio playing and I heard an announcement that Charles and Francis Hunter, evangelists who were anointed to pray for healing for the sick and who felt led to train others who felt called to a healing ministry, were coming to a city near ours. The announcer stated that they wanted to specifically pray for couples who were barren so that they could conceive a child. My heart leapt within me, and I said, "I am going to be there when they come, no matter what!!!" I talked to other people in our church and we got a big group of people to go together so we could all learn more about healing. Talk about excited!!! I couldn't wait!!! This was what I had prayed for and here it was!!! Praise God!!!

So we went to the sessions at the big church in October (one month before November with no baby in sight except for our brother and sister-in-law's), and I kept waiting for the moment when I would be led to go forward to have them lay hands on me and pray for me to conceive. It was the first morning session and they were calling people forward for prayer. Suddenly

I heard the Lord speak to me and say, "Do not go up there. Stay where you are!" I was astounded. I couldn't believe what I had just heard! "How can this be? I have waited and waited for so long, and now this huge NO from You, God!" I felt that I was going to faint. My hopes were dashed. Total despair gripped me. Had I just read what I wanted to read into this? Was I trying to manipulate God to do things the way I wanted Him to do things? I gave up, right then and there. I just wanted to go home and cry myself into oblivion.

But God....oh, but God! He had a Plan alright, just as He said through the prophet in Jeremiah 29:11 (NIV), [11] For I know the plans I have for you," declares the LORD, "plans to prosper you and not to harm you, plans to give you hope and a future." When the first session came to an end, they called for a break, then reconvened to do something totally different. They had a panel of people from various vocations come to the platform and answer questions about the healing ministry. One of them was a quiet, meek chiropractor from a nearby metropolis who just seemed to have a huge heart of compassion for people who were hurting. I felt very drawn to hang on every word he spoke. When the panel session was finished, the Hunters announced that each panel member would come down to the audience level and pray for anyone that needing healing. Well, this time, I got the green light! "Yes, let him pray for you," I heard God say in that still small voice. So after a few men and women had been prayed for, it was my turn. I briefly told him that my husband and I had prayed for and believed for a baby for years with no success. He immediately, with such quiet yet powerful authority, held up his hand and said, "People, pray." I will never forget that moment in time. Everyone in this intimate circle prayed in such unity in God's Spirit as he laid his hands on my head, and I slumped to the ground in a heap. I just lay there in such surrender, such peace, such assurance that our prayers had been answered.

Well, it came time for my in-laws to have their third baby. They asked me to come to their home to take care of their other two children while she was in the hospital, and I was more than happy to help them. Randy and I had some sweet time together before I left to go to the city where they lived, not knowing how long I would be gone on this mission of love.

Once I arrived at their home, we had one false start the first night, but the second night was the real thing and we were all blessed to welcome their third child, their second little baby boy.

Guess what!!! August 20th, exactly nine months to the day from their blessed arrival, our home was blessed with our own perfect little girl, Elizabeth Anne Blankenship. Just as God had said, we DID have a baby in November. She was just extremely tiny and safely tucked in the inner sanctum of my womb at the time. God hears our prayers. And He answers them in His Way, in His Timing.

Now, as you may recall, Elizabeth in the New Testament was the elderly barren wife of Zacharias, one of the priests of the Lord. God spoke to her husband as he was serving in the Temple and told him that his wife would, against all odds, conceive and bare a son, and guess what!!! She did, and that baby's life helped changed the world. His name was John the Baptist, the cousin and forerunner of Joseph and Mary's son Jesus, our Savior.

And Hannah (the Hebrew form of the name Anna from which we derived Beth's middle name Anne), who was the second wife of Elkanah and who was also barren, had to bear up under the painful taunting of his first wife Peninah who had many children. But Hannah believed against all odds, and prayed and made a vow that if God would remember her and give her a son she would dedicate him to the Lord for his entire life. And guess what!!! He did, and she did, and Samuel became one of the most important and powerful prophets of God who ever lived.

You need to know that Elizabeth and Hannah and I had become great buddies by the time our beautiful Elizabeth Anne was brought into our lives. I had meditated on the scriptures surrounding their lives for years. And the one that dear Hannah gave me, which is framed and hung on our hallway wall with a picture of our Beth is this: "27 For this child I prayed, and the LORD has given me my petition which I asked of Him. 28 So I have also dedicated her to the LORD; as long as she lives she is dedicated to the LORD." 1 Samuel 1:27-28 (NASB)

Now I KNOW that there are situations in which God answers our prayers in a totally different way than the way we have asked Him to do. I've read many true stories about couples who have prayed for a child and who never had one by natural means. However, God gave them either one or more adopted children, or a child to mentor and encourage in their faith as they grew, and, oh, what a blessing His Plan became to them. In His infinite Wisdom and Love a different and special kind of family was what He had in mind for these couples.

So, I urge you to be sensitive to what other people are going through in life, whether it concerns childlessness or singleness or with whatever issue they're dealing. Do not make assumptions or statements that may be hurtful, but pray and ask God to bless them with His perfect Will and Plan for their lives.

Psalm 69:16 (AMP) Answer me, O Lord, for Your lovingkindness is sweet *and* good *and* **comforting**; According to the greatness of Your compassion, turn to me.

2 Corinthians 1:3-5 (NASB)-- ³ Blessed *be* the God and Father of our Lord Jesus Christ, the Father of mercies and **God of all comfort**, ⁴ **Who comforts us** in all our affliction so that **we will be able to comfort those who are in any affliction with the comfort with which we ourselves are comforted by God.** ⁵ For just as the sufferings of Christ are ours in abundance, **so also our comfort is abundant through Christ.**

Oh, Amen and Amen!

BIG DAY AT THE PARK

Years and years ago, God gave me a vision concerning how He works many times in our lives when He has made a Promise to us in His Word and we make the choice to have faith to believe that it will come to pass. It goes something like this:

A loving mother tells her little boy that this coming Friday they are going to go to his favorite park together to play. The little guy is absolutely elated at the awesome news and can think of little else. Due to his age, he does not yet understand the true nature of time, so the first morning after the big announcement he jumps out of bed and runs to His Mother with a huge smile on his face. He holds onto her legs, looks up at her and exuberantly asks, "Mommy, Mommy, are we going to the park today?" She bends down to look lovingly into his eyes and answers, "No, not today, darling, but I promise that we ARE going to the park **on Friday.**" He looks a bit surprised but accepts His Mom's words and goes on with the activities of the day.

The next day, he leaps out of bed and again runs through the house until he finds his Mommy and asks the same question, "Are we going to the park TODAY? You SAID we are going to the park on Friday!" She picks him up in her arms and gives him a big hug, and tells him, "No, my sweet child, today is not Friday, but I told you we are going, and we WILL go to the park **on FRIDAY.** You can count on it!" He gets that look on his face that says, "I believe you, but this is harder than I thought it was going to be." Then he runs off to play.

On the third morning, he simply puts one foot at a time on the floor and walks through the house and asks with less enthusiasm, "Is THIS the day, Mommy?" She knows what he's going through, gets down on her knees and kisses his little cheek and says, "You and I have got some important things to do BEFORE we go to the park **this Friday**, but we ARE going to go, for sure! Trust me, honey!" He walks off dejectedly and almost decides that it's really not going to ever happen, EXCEPT for the fact that he knows his Mom always tells him the truth, and has a track record to back it up.

The next morning, with almost every smidgeon of excitement gone but holding onto the little bit of assurance he has left, he trudges through the house, sees his Mommy doing laundry, walks up to her and slowly says, "Mommy, this isn't the day, is it?" And with such pure joy she picks him up and spins him around with a huge smile on her face and ecstatically tells him, "YES, THIS IS THE DAY? **THIS IS FRIDAY**, THE DAY I PROMISED YOU WE WOULD GO TO THE PARK, AND WE <u>ARE</u> GOING, JUST LIKE I SAID!" The look on his face is priceless! With those huge expectant eyes and his mouth in the shape of a big round O, he squeals in delight which gives her such joy! He can hardly believe it's really happening...the reward of believing the words his dear Mommy had spoken to him "such a long, long time ago," the promised end of his faith, the blessing of sticking with it because he knew the one he had believed and was positively persuaded that she was able to keep that which he had committed unto her against that day.

Psalm 113:9 (NAS)-- "For He makes the barren woman abide in the house as a joyful mother of children."

Thank You, Lord, for fulfilling Your Word that we believed concerning the birth of our children.

Thank You for helping us to persevere and for fulfilling the verse that says in Psalm 126:6 (MSG)

4-6 "And now, GOD, do it again—bring rains to our drought-stricken lives so those who planted their crops in despair will shout hurrahs at the harvest, So those who went off with heavy hearts will come home laughing, with armloads of blessing."

Friday came! Hallelujah!!!

Believe God's Promises, and believe that Friday will come for you...in God's timing. TGIF!!!

FORGIVENESS

As we all know, there are going to be people and situations in our lives that offend and hurt us, and if we allow them to do so, can cause a root of bitterness to rise up in our hearts and minds, consuming our thoughts like corrosive acid, causing even more harm, not to the offender, but to us, the offended one. Unforgiveness, bitterness, resentment, anger, and even murderous thoughts can begin to build evil strongholds in our lives, and can affect us spiritually, emotionally, mentally and yes, physically; not at all what Jesus meant when He said in John 10:10 (AMP)-- [10] The thief comes only in order to steal and kill and destroy. **I came that they may have *and* enjoy life, and have it in abundance** [to the full, till it overflows].

Well, I've certainly had my share of hurts and offenses, just as you probably have, and many times I have not handled them well at all. One day several years ago, I had a vision concerning this important area of our lives. I had been hearing for years that we have got to make the conscious decision to give the offender over to the Lord, to let HIM handle them and change their hearts. I had been trying to do that, without much success. So….I saw myself, standing there in this vision with me carrying the person who had hurt me in my arms. I walked over to a sheer cliff, knowing full well that Jesus was standing at the bottom of the precipice waiting for me to let the perpetrator go, for that person to fall down into His arms. However, the person was totally unaware that Jesus was down at the bottom of that cliff. I said to him/ her, "I forgive you," and let them drop, knowing Jesus would catch them as they screamed and flailed in terror as they fell. But….I did what I was supposed to do, right?! It gave me a sense of satisfaction that I had put them in the arms of the Great Forgiver of our souls, for a minute. I knew deep down inside that this was not what Jesus had in mind… not at all.

So, a couple of years later, there was a sequel to this vision. Still dealing with the same people as before (because my fleshly methods had brought no resolution whatever to the problems I had with them), I held one of them in my arms, said "I forgive you," then promptly and gently handed them over into the caring arms of our Lord Who was standing right in front of me, looking lovingly into my eyes, which I certainly did not deserve (I believe that would be called Grace). He held them close in His unconditional Love, and in His infinite Wisdom, and dealt with their issues. SO much better than my little carnal picture of forgiving. Thank You, Lord!

One of our dear employees once gave me such insight and Godly advice in this area. She told me that she was able to consistently forgive someone in her life due to the fact that she realized that this person dealt with mental health issues. I thought about this over and over and came to the conclusion that every one of us on planet earth deals with "mental health issues" to some degree or another, and many times the person we are having a hard time with actually has the same issues we are dealing with ourselves. That's hard to come to grips with but it is so true. So when God showed me the sequel to the first vision on forgiveness, He expounded on it through a sweet sister to help me really "get" it. He's so awesome!

In Matthew 6:14-15 (AMP), Jesus tells us this: "¹⁴ For if you forgive others their trespasses [their reckless and willful sins], your heavenly Father will also forgive you. ¹⁵ But if you do not forgive others [nurturing your hurt and anger with the result that it interferes with your relationship with God], then your Father will not forgive your trespasses." Yeowwww!!! That's big!!!

³²⁻³⁵ "The king summoned the man and said, 'You evil servant! I forgave your entire debt when you begged me for mercy. Shouldn't you be compelled to be merciful to your fellow servant who asked for mercy?' The king was furious and put the screws to the man until he paid back his entire debt. And that's exactly what my Father in heaven is going to do to each one of you who doesn't forgive unconditionally anyone who asks for mercy." This is God's Word from Matthew 18:34-35 (MSG) and we have got to take this matter seriously. He means business!

How many of us have had THIS happen to us as a result of unforgiveness... those unrelenting, torturous thoughts that no one else is experiencing but you, because you won't forgive? No, this is NOT the abundant life Jesus promised....far from it indeed. But the good thing is, from the mouth of Jesus in John 8:31-32, "If you abide in My Word, you are truly disciples of Mine; and you shall know the Truth, and the Truth shall make you free." Yes!! That's a Promise we can take to the bank!!!

Just a word of caution to all those who will hear: We may have to do this more than once with that very same person or persons, as Jesus told Peter in Matthew 18:21-23 in the Amplified version "[21] Then Peter came up to Him and said, 'Lord, how many times may my brother sin against me and I forgive him *and* let it go? [As many as] up to seven times?' [22] Jesus answered him, 'I tell you, not up to seven times, but **seventy times seven**!'" Seventy times seven??!!! Ouch!! As they say in the sports world, "Just do it"!!! It pays heavenly dividends.

THE BODY OF CHRIST

My husband Randy and I serve in a powerful Christian ministry. We both attended our first weekends in the spring of 2002, and it has been an extremely effective tool God has used to change our hearts and lives, as well as those of thousands and thousands of men and women across the globe. We feel blessed to be a part of such an incredible ministry.

The very first weekend I served, I had a break from my duties which enabled me to sit in the auditorium and listen to one of the talks given by lay people and clergy, just as I had listened to all the talks as a candidate on my first weekend. One of the things that had struck me so profoundly on that first weekend was the fact that these men and women, who seemed to have it all together and looked as if everything had always been either normal or better than that, had stories to tell of heart-wrenching experiences that should have destroyed their faith and turned them away from God. Instead, through all the tragedies I had listened to on both weekends, their faith was increased and they had an even stronger and more intimate relationship with the Lord than they had had prior to the hard times about which they spoke.

I had heard testimonies throughout my life similar to these, but when you have the time to listen to one after the other after the other in one relatively short period of time, it all starts to come together in a cohesive theme… "God Who is God of the mountains is still God of the valleys in our lives". It's true. It's life changing to come to that realization.

As I sat there by myself in the back of the room, suddenly it was as if I could see the arms and nail-pierced hands of Jesus Himself, spreading out wider and wider to encompass the room full of candidates and servants. Then He spoke something that rocked my world. He said, "THIS (all of these hurting and bruised and healed survivors of countless battles) is My Body, which is broken for you." What!!! I had NEVER thought about that statement as anything other than Jesus' Words concerning His OWN physical body which we all know was so unbelievably and savagely beaten and torn by the Roman soldiers. I had never imagined that it included those of us who make up the Church, the Body of Christ. But He WAS including all of us who have asked Him to be our Lord and Savior, who have gone through awful and heart-breaking events, many of which have gone untold through the years because of the shame, grief and fear involved. We, also, are that broken bread and that poured out wine when we submit our griefs to Him, to be used to bring encouragement and new life to others who are now going through the tough times of life.

There is a scripture from Revelation 12:11 which I have grown to love and it states this in the Living Bible Translation, "[11] They defeated him (Satan) by the blood of the Lamb and by their testimony; for they did not love their lives but laid them down for him." Oh my goodness, this scripture was being fulfilled right in front of me, in my sight and in my hearing, as yet another testimony spoke so profoundly of the Faithful Love of God in our lives to lift us up from the ash heap and give us new life. What an awesome God we serve, and what an incredible blessing to serve alongside and help fellow sojourners overcome seemingly insurmountable obstacles on this sometimes treacherous path we call life. What an honor to not only say, "I can only imagine," but "I KNOW what you're going through. I've been there, too." God bless the sometimes pain-filled, broken road, that led me straight to You, dear Lord.

THE BEST FERTILIZER EVER!

Several years ago, after Randy and I had been serving in the Christian weekends I have mentioned in past chapters, I was asked to be one of the speakers at the upcoming women's weekend. Oh my goodness, talk about fear setting in as I pondered getting up in front of all those dear ladies whom I was sure expected to have a "good" speaker enlighten them on the subject of Piety. Piety!!! I really had no idea, at least no accurate idea, as to what that word even meant. I thought it meant living with a "better than thou" attitude. And they expected me to talk about this illusive subject for 40 long minutes!!! How in the world can anyone, especially me, hold people's attention for 40 minutes on a subject that sounded as interesting as watching paint dry?

Well, I was stuck. And being such a novice to things such as emails with attachments back then, I had no clue that I had been given an actual outline with suggestions on how to go about talking about Piety (which by the way means living your life with your focus on God). Soooooo....off I went, struggling every step of the way, even to the point of getting shingles from stressing over this dreaded talk, and having computer problems on top of all that! Super!!! (I hope and pray that none of you ever, ever contracts this awful disease, so let me advise you to stay so in tune with the Lord so that stress does not reach that point in your mind and body).

I started digging through Christian books I had around the house, trying my best to come up with enough stuff to entertain people for two-thirds of an hour, all to no avail. It was hopeless. I felt as if I had been thrown overboard from a ship in the middle of the ocean with a scrawny piece of driftwood as my only life saver. "HELP!!!!" I cried!!! "Where are You, God!!! I need You desperately!!!"

Then one day, that still small voice spoke to me. That reminds me of the time that our oldest daughter was in first grade. I came to her class one day just as all the children were coming in from recess, all red-faced and sweaty, and loud. Beth's teacher sat down at her desk, and quietly spoke these words almost in a whisper, "Boys and girls, it's time to sit down and stop talking." And they actually heard her, in the middle of the chaos, and sat down at their desks and closed their mouths. I was absolutely astonished. How in the world did she do that?!!! How did they hear her? A history of respect and authority had already been established in this classroom and the evidence was as clear as it could be. These little children knew her voice, and knew she meant business, for their good.

It's just like the parable of the Good Shepherd in John 10: 1-5, 14-16 (AMP)-- "I assure you *and* most solemnly say to you, he who does not enter by the door into the sheepfold, but climbs up from some other place [on the stone wall], that one is a thief and a robber. ²But he who enters by the door is the shepherd of the sheep [the protector and provider]. ³The doorkeeper opens [the gate] for this man, **and the sheep hear his voice *and* pay attention to it. And [knowing that they listen] he calls his own sheep by name and leads them out [to pasture].** ⁴When he has brought all his own *sheep* outside, he walks on ahead of them, **and the sheep follow him because they know his voice *and* recognize his call. ⁵They will never follow a stranger, but will run away from him, because they do not know the voice of strangers.**"

¹⁴**I (Jesus) am the Good Shepherd, and I know [without any doubt those who are] My own and My own know Me [and have a deep, personal relationship with Me]—** ¹⁵even as the Father knows Me and I know the Father—and I lay down My [very own] life [sacrificing it] for *the benefit of* the sheep. ¹⁶**I have other sheep [beside these] that are not of this fold. I must bring those also, and they will listen to My voice *and* pay attention to My call, and they will become one flock with one Shepherd.**

So, as I continued to struggle with this challenging talk, that still small voice spoke this word to me, "Compost." "Compost?" I said, not having a clue as to why God would say that to me at that frantic point in my life.

"Yes, compost." I sat there and waited to see what possible explanation might come forth. And then awesome God said this to me, "When you take all the garbage and old newspapers with stories about you that you wish no one knew anything about and that you wish you could forget because of the pain and the shame you experience when you remember all that junk, and let Me put it out in the chicken-wired compost pile in the backyard of your life, in the heat of the Son of God, THEN I can take that smelly, slimy stuff and turn it into the best fertilizer on the planet. I can use it to grow the seeds of Truth I have planted in your heart and give you a testimony that will blow people away with My Power to transform a life that is hopeless and purposeless and floating on the sea of despair with only a scrawny piece of driftwood between you (or them) and the hungry sharks that are waiting to devour you.

And I thought about all the talks I had heard other ladies give on past weekends, ladies who looked as if they had never had a care in the world, and who had, as we learned while listening to their talks, been through such horrendous "garbage" that could have destroyed them. I had sat in amazement as we realized, story after story, what God had done in His compassion and love to rescue them from their own destructions, wrong choices, evil people's plans for them, and Satan's organized schemes to destroy them. Compost! Yes!!! Fertilizer that God used to make them grow, and to facilitate growth in those who heard their stories. Wow!!! Who would have thought?!!

Listen to this in Revelation 12:11 (AMP)--**And they overcame _and_ conquered him (Satan)** because of the blood of the Lamb and **because of the word of their testimony**, for they did not love their life _and_ renounce their faith even when faced with death.

Let God take that ole stinky compost pile and turn it into the sweetest smelling perfume, a delightful fragrance that wafts its way into the Heavenly throne room of God's Presence for Him to use for His eternal Purposes to transform lives for all eternity. He, the Creator, knows what and how to do it. And He will... when we let Him.

THE REDWOOD FOREST

Back in 2002, my dear Mom was one of many winners in a contest held by her bank nationwide for employees who were instrumental in selling the most CDs and other banking products. My Mom was always one of the hardest working people I ever knew, and a real asset to any business for which she worked. Well, she and the guest of her choice were blessed with an all expenses paid trip to San Francisco, California, and guess who she chose to be her guest……me!!!! I could hardly believe it! I had never been to California and could hardly wait to board that plane with my sweet friend and companion, my Mom.

There was a hurricane brewing on the east coast on that day, and the cloud cover from that huge storm absolutely engulfed our great country….until we got about midway across the United States. The clouds parted like the Red Sea, and there it was, a picture of some of the most inhospitable terrain I had ever seen, endless desert and seemingly impenetrable mountain ranges. My admiration for the brave men and women who pioneered this land grew by the minute as we flew over the incomprehensible span of the beautiful but treacherous Grand Canyon and the Sierra Nevada Mountains. What an experience!!!

Well, upon our much anticipated arrival in San Francisco, the nationally known bank for which my Mom worked graciously and generously arranged for us to stay in the Westin Saint Frances Hotel, right in the middle of downtown San Francisco. This was the hotel in which President Ronald Reagan and Queen Elizabeth had met years before, so you can only imagine the beauty of the décor and architecture of this grand accommodation. They treated us like royalty, every meal a culinary delight with the freshest of locally grown food, and the tables and ballrooms decorated beyond our imagination. We were given free sight-seeing tours and made every effort to explore everything we had time to see in the days we were there. Mom and I would just pinch ourselves and ask, "Is this real? Why are they doing this for us (especially me)?" It was a time I will absolutely never forget the rest of my life.

We traveled to Twin Peaks, China Town (several times—we loved it!), the Golden Gate Bridge, Sausalito, Lombard Street and Fisherman's Wharf, and several other well known landmarks. But I have to tell you that for me, the most life-changing trip we took was out to the Redwood Forest, discovered by John Muir, the great naturalist. We had no idea what an impact this great monument to our Creator would make on our lives. Unless you have been there for yourself, it is impossible to explain to anyone just how enormous these giant trees really are, making one feel infinitesimally small in comparison to their great stature.

The highlight for me was listening to the park ranger tell all who would stop and listen about several of the trees' unique features. This became quite a spiritual experience and something that, I soon realized, if we choose to apply the lessons learned from these silent but divinely-designed life forms, we might all do much better in life.

She explained that in this area of the country there is very little annual rainfall, which in itself is an amazing fact considering the enormity of the need for water for these great giants. She told us that fog is their main source of hydration, and that the tiny needles of their branches are like little "catchers" of the droplets drifting through the air as the fog silently passes their way. The drops of water are then absorbed by the needles, thus providing the trees' unquenchable need for this life-giving substance. I was absolutely floored by this information.

The ranger then related to us that although their seeds are the primary means of reproduction, they also have a very interesting way to duplicate themselves through their very unsightly burls. These are big, ugly, gnarly growths on the sides of their trunks that continue to grow out and then downward until they touch the earth and establish a root system to begin a brand new tree, but which is still connected to the host tree. Unbelievable!!!

Going on with her incredible facts, she explained that with the enormous weight and height of the redwoods, maintaining their stance in the forest floor might be a problem except for this: although their root system is very shallow (which is hard to believe), they have been designed to intertwine their roots with the roots of all the surrounding redwoods, thereby supporting and holding each other up through the strongest winds and storms. How awesome is that?!!! Now this is not to say that through natural processes the trees do not fall on occasion. But even this event provides those who see them an even more astounding revelation of their greatness. One of the felled trees which had landed across the path had been sawed in two places in order to clear the pathway for visitors to the park. The giant had then been marked by park rangers with dates pinpointing the time frame of its rings, the most astounding being the birth of Jesus Christ as one of those events, more than 2000 years ago!!! How humbling and awe-inspiring to stand there looking at a tangible form that had been alive when Jesus lived on the earth!!! What an incredible God we serve!!! What a perfect Creator, to have thought of everything that just these beautiful specimens would need to survive through all these centuries.

Well, as I mentioned earlier, a spirit of awe and worship came over me as I gazed up into these magnificent creations. The thought occurred to me that while we are walking through this life, sometimes as if in a dry and parched land, when we make the effort to stop, to stand, to look up and stretch our arms to the heavens in reverence and praise, we can "catch" those precious drops of the Water of the Word of God in the cloud of His Presence. I am learning that this is the only thing that can truly quench our tired and thirsty souls, and make the difference that we all long for on our journeys here on this beautiful sphere we call earth.

Then there are, as will inevitably occur if we live long enough, those hard to explain, tough events in our lives, those terrible ugly burls that seem to come out of nowhere. These are events which we absolutely cannot understand at the time, which may even cause us to question whether God sees or cares about what's happening in our lives, or if He really exists. But be encouraged…IF we will choose to wait patiently upon the Lord, and not lean on our own understanding, but humbly trust in His infinite

Wisdom and Goodness, He WILL turn those awful, gnarly times in our lives into a brand new way of living, full of His Life and abundance, rooted and grounded in His abiding Love. THAT'S when He can use us to the utmost to minister to others in need!!!

And, my friends, during those tough times in life when the height and the weight of our life problems become seemingly too much to bear and we know that we are getting ready to fall, then we must, as members of the Body of Christ, humble ourselves and reach out with our roots firmly established in God's Word and support each other in prayer, in fellowship, in encouragement, in comfort, in Godly counsel, and in Christian service. That's when we'll realize that we are fulfilling the two greatest commandments: To love the Lord our God with all our hearts, and minds and souls,….and to love our neighbors as ourselves. What an incredible Plan God has for His dear People, and what a wonderful picture He has given us through His Creation, to show us through natural parables how to live this life He has given us. And to see Jesus born anew in our hearts…every day, on **every** ring.

Now let God's Word speak for itself:

Isaiah 61:1-4 (NASB)--The Spirit of the Lord GOD is upon me, because the LORD has anointed me to bring good news to the afflicted; He has sent me to bind up the brokenhearted, to proclaim liberty to captives and freedom to prisoners; [2] to proclaim the favorable year of the LORD and the day of vengeance of our God; to comfort all who mourn, [3] to grant those who mourn *in* Zion, giving them a garland instead of ashes, the oil of gladness instead of mourning, the mantle of praise instead of a spirit of fainting. **So they will be called oaks of righteousness, the planting of the LORD, that He may be glorified.** [4] Then they will rebuild the ancient ruins, they will raise up the former devastations; and they will repair the ruined cities, the desolations of many generations.

THE BRIGHTNESS OF HIS GLORY

It was February 5, 1984, 7:15 AM. I was sound asleep. Then I heard my name called audibly two times. At first I thought it was my husband Randy playing a trick on me, but Randy was obviously deep in sleep. I felt like Samuel in the Old Testament (read 1 Samuel chapter 3) when he was a little boy serving Eli in the Temple. The Lord instructed me to go into our living room where there was a wall of windows facing toward the east, covered with white sheer curtains. The sun was just beginning to come up in the east through the trees, and all I could see was one very bright spot of sunlight at that point in time. The Lord said to me, "Do you see the brightness of My Glory?"…..three times. I answered yes each time. He then said, "Get down on your knees with your face to the floor," which I did. He followed with instructions to get back up on the couch. When I did so, then opened my eyes, the entire room was filled with an incredible, brilliant misty light, even where there should have been dark shadows. He spoke many times, "Remember the brightness of My Glory." I told him over and over that I would but did not understand what any of this meant.

I then went into another room to read my Bible. The chapter I was on in my journey of reading through the Bible "just happened" to be Ezekiel 43:1-2, 4-7a (NASB), which amazingly said, "Then he led me to the gate, the gate facing toward the east; and behold the Glory of the God of Israel was coming from the way of the east, and I fell on my face. And the Glory of The Lord came into the house, and behold, the Glory of The Lord filled the house. And he said to me, 'This is the place of the soles of My feet. This is the law of the house; its entire area on the top of the mountain all around shall be most holy.'"

Whoa!!!! Awesome….but I still had no idea what any of that meant. We went to church that morning. The pastor preached from Isaiah 60:1-3 (AMP) "Arise [from spiritual depression to a new life], shine [be radiant with the glory *and* brilliance of the LORD]; for your light has come, and the glory *and* brilliance of the LORD has risen upon you. ² For in fact, darkness will cover the earth and deep darkness *will cover* the peoples; but the LORD will rise upon you and His glory *and* brilliance will be seen on you. ³ Nations will come to your light, and kings to the brightness of your rising." Incredible, but I still didn't get it!

A dear friend of mine, Susan, whom I had told about this unforgettable event, came up to me one Sunday, and said, "I think I know what that was about." She said, "Read Hebrews 1:1-3." (NKJV). So I did. "God, who at various times and in various ways spoke in time past to the fathers by the prophets, ² has in these last days spoken to us by **_His_ Son**, **whom He has appointed heir of all things**, through whom also He made the worlds; ³ **Who being the brightness of _His_ glory** and the express image of His person, and upholding all things by the word of His power, when He had by Himself purged our sins, sat down at the right hand of the Majesty on high."

"So", I thought, "Okay, the brightness of His Glory is Jesus," but I still didn't see how that applied to my life.

At an intercessory prayer meeting at a church we attended years ago, as I prayed I had what I would call a vision in which a huge object, the shape of what I would call a nuclear power plant but was made entirely of a brilliant light which was shining in the darkness, was drawing people from all over the area in which we live. I could not tell its location exactly, but I knew in my spirit that it was in this area where we lived, and that multitudes of people, young and old, were coming to this object of light.

Then a few years ago, at the closing of one of the Christian women's weekend on which I served, as we all stood in a circle around the room singing that timeless hymn "Amazing Grace," I heard that still small voice say to me, "This is it." I answered, "This is it? This is what?" Then He said, "The Brightness of My Glory." Whoa, I said once again, still not understanding the implications of this statement.

As I served on yet another weekend (sometimes I'm kind of slow), I realized something I had never understood before. When we serve the Lord in

ANY venue, one in spirit with Him, serving an audience of One, we are essentially being Jesus, The Word of God, made manifest in the flesh to those we are serving. These people are seeing and experiencing Jesus' Love, His Ways, His Words, His Actions before their very eyes…. through us. We, as His "re-presentors", are being Jesus to them, in a real and tangible way. He has become, through our submission, our obedience and our service, the Brightness of God's Glory shining in a very dark world that needs to know Him, His Love, and the Power of His Resurrection…. through our lives. Like moths to the light at night.

Matthew 5:14-15 (NASB)-- [14] "**You are the light of the world**. A city set on a hill cannot be hidden; [15] nor does *anyone* light a lamp and put it under a basket, but on the lampstand, and it gives light to all who are in the house."

HIDE IT UNDER A BUSHEL….NO….
I'M GONNA LET IT SHINE!!!

THE EAGLE

Several years ago, as I mentioned previously, I was serving on a Christian Women's weekend (Randy, of course, serves on the Men's weekends) in a very active position as the head of one of the serving teams. It was, at it always is, a power-filled, life-changing weekend for the candidates as well as for each member of the team. That Sunday afternoon, as the weekend came to a glorious close, I was very fatigued and ready for my dear husband Randy to come and help me finish packing up all my gear as he has always done so faithfully. But as I walked out of the dorm I checked my cell phone and saw the text he had sent saying that he was with his mother who was in the hospital and would not be able to come to the campground. "Oh my goodness," I thought. "I can't do this! I am just too tired to be able to go around to the different buildings and gather all my stuff and pack it in my car. Oh, God, what am I going to do? I'm one of the very last people on the campus so there's no one who can help me. PLEASE, HELP ME, LORD!!!"

I began to walk across the parking lot toward the farthest building where some of my belongings were waiting for me, dragging my feet as I plodded along, feeling pretty sorry for myself, I must admit. In that moment of seeming impossibility to carry out a simple but daunting task, I had a decision to make.......would I do this in my own strength, which was next to nothing, or would I draw upon the strength of God which I knew came from the eternal Blood Covenant and through His everlasting Promises? The first choice didn't make any sense at all since I really could not do it, so I asked the Lord for some Encouragement from His Word, the Bible. The thought came to me instantly from Isaiah 40: 28-31 (KJV) which says so beautifully,

[28] "Have you not known? Have you not heard? The everlasting God, the Lord, the Creator of the ends of the earth, does not faint or grow weary;

there is no searching of His understanding. ²⁹ He gives power to the faint *and* weary, and to him who has no might He increases strength [causing it to multiply and making it to abound]. ³⁰ Even the youths shall faint and be weary, and the young men shall utterly fall: ³¹ But they that wait upon the LORD shall renew their strength; **they shall mount up with wings as eagles**; they shall run, and not be weary; and they shall walk, and not faint."

I began to speak this awesome Promise of God out loud, over and over, and started to feel my strength being restored even as I spoke. And then, as our Heavenly Father is SO good to do, He did something that almost blew my mind. As I walked from the parking lot through an opening in a six foot wall, headed toward the building where my things were stacked up, I looked up above the chapel right in front of me (the chapel that is no longer there and thus holds an even more special place in my heart), and there, circling in majestic glory was a mature bald eagle with wings spread out to catch the slightest wind allowing him to effortlessly float, as it were, above that place of worship. A huge smile came to my face and God's strength was infused into my beleaguered body, allowing me to seemingly float around the campus to finish all that I had begun three days earlier. I WILL NEVER FORGET THE VISION THAT GOD SHOWED ME THAT DAY, once I "died to myself" and let His Resurrection Power fill me up as It has done so many times in the past.

I would like to share with you some verses that I pray have a lasting impact in your life. Please read this one that holds such a special place in my heart:

Psalm 103: 1-5 (NASB) Bless the LORD, O my soul, and all that is within me, *bless* His holy name. ² Bless the LORD, O my soul, and forget none of His benefits; ³ Who pardons all your iniquities, Who heals all your diseases; ⁴ Who redeems your life from the pit, Who crowns you with lovingkindness and compassion; ⁵ Who satisfies your years with good things, **so *that* your youth is renewed like the eagle.**

Years ago, when our youngest daughter Grace was a child, she and I would always quote two scriptures together before she went to sleep at night. One of them was from Psalm 4:8 (KJV)—"I will both lay me down in peace and sleep, for Thou Lord only makest me to dwell in safety." The other was from Psalm 103 as quoted above. I was so curious about what it meant when it said in the King James Version, "so that your youth is renewed like the eagle's." I had no clue as to its meaning, so, as I have made it a habit to do, and the Lord has been so faithful to answer, I asked Him what that meant. It took a little while, but one morning as I was watching one of my favorite Christian television teachers, she said something that totally captured my attention. The Lord had put in her heart a curiosity about the birds named in the Bible, and the very first one on her list was the eagle (funny how that happened). Through her research she had found that when an eagle, which is a bird of prey, cannot find a live animal to swoop down upon to eat, it will resort to eating a dead carcass. Now, if that animal has been dead for too long a time and is toxic to the eagle, that God-inspired bird will fly as high as its strength allows to a tall tree or cliff, spread its wings in the presence of the sun and let the heat and light of that celestial being bake out any and all poison from its system. What a picture of how God has instilled in our hearts to do the same when people or circumstances have poisoned our hearts and minds. He draws us to come up with Him as high as our strength allows and spread our arms in total worship and submission to Him in the Heat and Light of the Presence of His Son. Then, as we allow Him to, He bakes out of each one of us all that would destroy us, and renews our strength once again. What an awesome God we serve!!!

A TRUE STORY OF A 300 YEAR OLD PRAYER

When our dear friends, the Reid family, moved to Gainesville, Florida, some 30 years ago, we would often times drive the 2 hours up I-75 to visit with them and go to many exciting football and volleyball games there at the university. We so enjoyed being with them and staying in their beautiful and welcoming home. They truly have the gift of hospitality, not just to us but to SO many through the years. What a blessing they are, indeed. True servants of the Lord with such giving hearts.

As I would always do as Doreen and I spent time preparing meals in their kitchen, I gazed at all the photos she had taped to the refrigerator and would ask, "Now who is this," and "who is that?" Each time Doreen would so sweetly explain that these family members were serving the Lord as missionaries, or in many other ways, in different places around the United States and the world.

I finally came to the point where I asked her, "Is everybody in your family saved and serving the Lord?" to which she, with her sweet voice and endearing smile, answered me all those years ago, "Yes, they are." I was astounded and said, "I don't think I know anybody that can say that their entire family has been saved and is serving the Lord. How do you all do that?" She then explained that her aunt had told her the story years ago of her genealogical search through Doreen's mother's side of the family.

She relayed to me that back in the 1700's, that great preacher Jonathan Edwards' (whose sermons on justification by faith in 1734 fueled the Great Awakening of 1739-1741 in New England, a fact I found in my own research on the subject) prayed together with his wife Sarah that every single one of their children and their descendants would be saved and serve the Lord. Now get this….Doreen's mother's side of the family are direct descendants of Jonathan and Sarah Edwards!!!! I was amazed…simply amazed!!! A prayer from more than 300 years ago was still in effect at the time Doreen told me this astounding story. The prayers of a loving father and mother, their dream and their vision for their children, have gone down, not just through the years or decades, but through the centuries, affecting their descendants and all whose lives they touch every day.

The cries of these dedicated parents were still being heard and answered by God Almighty. And His Word says in Acts 10:34 (KJV) that, "He is no respecter of persons." So....be encouraged as you pray for your loved ones in the days and years to come. God said in Isaiah 55:11 (AMP)-- **So will My word be which goes out of My mouth; It will not return to Me void** (useless, without result), **without accomplishing what I desire, and without succeeding *in the matter* for which I sent it**." Then, these powerful words "For I KNOW the Plans I have for you, plans to prosper you, not to harm you, Plans to give you a future and a hope," as divinely spoken by the prophet in Jeremiah 29:11 (NIV). Here's one I have loved so much from Isaiah 43:6 (AMP)—"I will say to the north, 'Give them up!' and to the south, 'Do not hold them back.' Bring my sons from far away and my daughters from the ends of the earth!" Take a look at this one in 2 Corinthians 1:20 (AMP): [20] "For as many as are the promises of God, **in Christ** they are [all answered] 'Yes.' So through Him we say our "Amen" to the glory of God." Yes, yes, and YES!!!

OH, HOW GREAT IS THY FAITHFULNESS,
OH GOD, MY FATHER!

THE WHIRLWIND

On Sunday morning, November 3rd, 1997, we at the church Randy and I were attending were gathered together for worship service, and held a special time of prayer for a mission team leaving from our church the following Thursday to travel to Guyana and Trinidad. The team was comprised of our pastor, a young man and two women from our fellowship. During the time of prayer, the Lord gave me a vision for the team who would be departing in a short time.

The vision was as follows: The mission team was caught up in a white whirlwind, in the eye of the whirling motion. Everywhere they "touched down" souls were being drawn up into the whirlwind from the bottom of the whirling which was shaped like a hollow tube instead of a thin cone shape one would normally think of while envisioning its shape. The souls were all being saved and delivered from demons who were being spun out of them into outer darkness. Meanwhile, God was pouring the Oil of the Holy Spirit so thickly onto the ones in the middle of the whirlwind that the oil spun out to touch and affect the lives of people they would not even see until they reached Heaven.

I was so excited about the vision that I asked God when I could share it with my friends. It was Wednesday, the day before the team departed that He gave me liberty to share with the intercessors at our prayer meeting what the vision had been. It was then that He showed me that it was not just for the team, but for all of us who have given Him our lives. A dear brother in Christ shared with me a scripture, Nahum 1:3 (AMP) which reads as follows: "The Lord is slow to anger and great in Power, and The Lord will by no means leave the guilty unpunished. **In whirlwind and storm** is His Way, and clouds are the dust beneath His feet." Well, this got me thinking that there were possibly other scriptures concerning whirlwinds and similar words other than the one I had read about Elijah in the past, so I set off to dig for the hidden treasure in God's Word, and these are the nuggets of gold I found as a result:

Genesis 1:1-3 (KJV)—In the beginning God created the Heaven and the earth. And the earth was without form, and void, and darkness was upon the face of the deep. And **the Spirit of God _moved_** (from the Hebrew word "racaph" which means **to brood, to flutter, to shake**) upon the face of the waters. And God said, "Let there be light, and there was light.

2 Kings 2:1 (KJV)—And it came about that when the Lord would take up Elijah by **a whirlwind** (from the Hebrew word "cereah" meaning hurricane, tempest, storm) to Heaven, that Elijah went with Elisha to Gilgal.

2 Kings 2:11 (KJV)— ¹¹ And it came to pass, as they still went on, and talked, that, behold, there appeared a chariot of fire, and horses of fire, and parted them both asunder; and Elijah went up **by a whirlwind** into heaven.

Please pay special attention in these next verses as to WHY the whirlwind "does its thing."

Job 37:2-13 (NASB)—Listen closely to the thunder of His voice, and the rumbling that goes out of His mouth. Under the whole Heaven He lets it loose, and His lightning to the ends of the earth. A voice roars; He thunders with His majestic voice, and He does not restrain the lightnings when His voice is heard. God thunders with His voice wondrously, doing great things which we cannot comprehend. For to the snow He says, 'Fall on the earth,' and to the downpour and the rain, 'Be strong.' He seals the hand of every man, **that all men may know His Word**. Then the beast goes into its lair, and remains in its den. Out of the south comes **the whirlwind**, and out of the north the cold. From the breath of God ice is made, and the expanse of the waters is frozen. Also with moisture he loads the thick cloud; He disperses the cloud of His lightning. And it changes direction, turning around by His guidance, that it may do whatever He commands it on the face of the inhabited earth. **Whether for correction, or for His world, or for loving-kindness, He causes it to happen.**

Word to the wise:

Job 38: 1-15 (NASB)—The the Lord answered Job out of **the whirlwind** and said, "Who is this that darkens counsel by words without knowledge? Now gird up your loins like a man, and I will ask you, and you instruct Me! Where were you when I laid the foundation of the earth? Tell Me, if you have understanding, who set its measurements, since you know? Or who laid its cornerstone, when the morning stars sang together, and all the sons of God shouted for joy? Or who enclosed the sea with doors, when, bursting forth, it went out from the womb; when I made a cloud its garment, and thick darkness its swaddling band, and I placed boundaries on it, and I set a bolt and doors, and I said, 'Thus far you shall come, but no farther; and here shall your proud waves stop?' Have you ever in your life commanded the morning, and caused the dawn to know its place; that it might take hold of the ends of the earth, and **the wicked be shaken out of it**? It is changed like clay under the seal; and they stand forth like a garment. And from the wicked their light is withheld, and the uplifted arm is broken."

Psalm 58: 6-11 (NASB)—O God, shatter the teeth of the wicked in their mouth; break out the fangs of the young lions, O Lord. Let them flow away like water that runs off; when he aims his arrows, let them be as headless shafts. Let them be as a snail which melts away as it goes along; like the miscarriages of a woman which never see the sun. Before your pots can feel the fire of thorns, He will sweep them away with **a whirlwind** (from the Hebrew word "saar"—to storm, to shiver *as demons do at the name of Jesus—italics are mine,* to be horribly afraid, fear, hurl as a storm, be tempestuous, come like or take away as with a whirlwind), the green and the burning alike. The righteous will rejoice when he sees the vengeance; he will wash his feet in the blood of the wicked. ***And men will say, "Surely there is a reward for the righteous; surely there is a God Who judges on earth!"***

Dear friends, do not reject the Wisdom that comes from God:

Proverbs 1:20-33 (NASB)—Wisdom shouts in the street, she lifts up her voice in the square; at the head of the noisy streets she cries out; at the entrance of the gates in the city, she utters her sayings, "How long, O naïve ones, will you love simplicity? And scoffers delight themselves in scoffing, and fools hate knowledge? Turn to my reproof, behold, I will pour out My Spirit on you; I will make My Words known to you. Because I called, and you refused; I stretched out My hand, and no one paid attention; and you neglected all My counsel, and did not want My reproof; I will even laugh at your calamity; I will mock when your dread comes, when your dread comes like **a storm** and your calamity comes on like **a whirlwind**, when distress and anguish come on you. Then they will call on Me, but I will not answer; they will seek me diligently, but they shall not find Me, because they hated knowledge, and did not choose the fear of The Lord. They would not accept My counsel. They spurned all My reproof. So they shall eat of the fruit of their own way, and be satiated with their own devices. For the waywardness of the naïve shall kill them, and the complacency of fools shall destroy them. *But he who listens to me (Wisdom) shall live securely, and shall be at ease from the dread of evil."*

Proverbs 10: 24-25 (NASB)—What the wicked fears will come upon him, and the desire of the righteous will be granted. When **the whirlwind** passes, the wicked is no more, *but the righteous has an everlasting foundation.* (What a Promise!)

The following sounds way too much like the United States of America today.

Isaiah 5:18-24, 26-30 (NASB)—Woe to those who drag iniquity with the cords of falsehood, and sin as if with cart ropes; who say, "Let Him make speed, let Him hasten his work, that we may see it; and let the purpose of the Holy One of Israel draw near and come to pass, that we may know it!" *Woe to those who call evil good, and good evil; who substitute darkness for light, and light for darkness; who substitute bitter for sweet, and sweet for bitter! Woe to those who are wise in their own eyes, and clever in their own sight! Woe to those who are heroes in drinking wine, and valiant men in mixing strong drink; who justify the wicked for a bribe, and take away the rights of the ones who are in the right!!! Therefore, as a tongue of fire consumes stubble, and dry grass collapses into the flame, so their root will become like rot and their blossom blow away as dust; for they have rejected the law of the Lord of Hosts, and despised the Word of the Holy One of Israel*.

He will also lift up a standard to the distant nation, and will whistle for it from the ends of the earth; and behold, it will come with speed swiftly. No one in it is weary or stumbles, none slumbers or sleeps; nor is the belt at its waist undone, nor its sandal strap broken. Its arrows are sharp, and all its bows are bent; the hoofs of its horses seem like flint, and **its chariot wheels like a whirlwind**. Its roaring is like a lioness, and it roars like young lions; it growls as it seizes the prey, and carries it off with no one to deliver it. And it shall growl over it in that day like the roaring of the sea. If one looks to the land, behold, there is darkness and distress; even the light is darkened by its clouds.

Woe be to those who persecute God's people!

Isaiah 17: 12-14 (NASB)—Alas, the uproar of many peoples who roar like the roaring of the seas, and the rumbling of nations who rush on like the rumbling of mighty waters! The nations rumble on like the rumbling of many waters, but He will rebuke them and they will flee far away, and be chased like chaff in the mountains before **the whirlwind**, or like **whirling dust before a gale**. At evening time, behold, there is terror! Before morning they are no more. *Such will be the portion of those who plunder us, and the lot of those who pillage (the Jews)*.

Beware, rulers and judges of nations!

Isaiah 40:21-26 (NASB)—Do you not know? Have you not heard? Has it not been declared to you from the beginning? Have you not understood from the foundations of the earth? It is He Who sits above the vault of the earth, and its inhabitants are like grasshoppers, Who stretches out the heavens like a curtain and spreads them out like a tent to dwell in. *He it is Who reduces rulers to nothing, Who makes the judges of the earth meaningless.* Scarcely have they been planted, scarcely have they been sown, scarcely has their stock taken root in the earth, but He merely blows on them, and they wither, and **the whirlwind carries them away like stubble**. To whom then will you liken Me that I should be his equal?

says the Holy One. Lift up your eyes on high and see Who has created the stars, the One Who leads forth their host by number, He calls them all by name; because of the greatness of His might and the strength of His power not one of them is missing.

Isaiah 41:13-16 (NASB)—"For I am the Lord your God, Who upholds your right hand, Who says to you, '*Do not fear, I will help you.*' Do not fear, you worm Jacob, you men of Israel; I will help you," declares the Lord, "and your Redeemer is the Holy One of Israel. Behold, I have made you a new, sharp threshing sledge with double edges; you will thresh the mountains, and pulverize them, and will make the hills like chaff. You will winnow them, and the wind will carry them away, and **the whirlwind will scatter them**; but you will rejoice in the Lord, you will glory in the Holy One of Israel."

Isaiah 66:15 (NASB)—**For behold The Lord will come in fire and His chariots like the whirlwind**, to render His anger with flames of fire.

Do not think that the wicked will forever get away with their wickedness!

Jeremiah 23: 19-22 (NASB)—Behold, **the whirlwind of the Lord** has gone forth in wrath, even **a whirling tempest**; **it will swirl down on the head of the wicked**. The anger of The Lord will not turn back until He has performed and carried out the purposes of His heart; in the last days you will clearly understand it. I did not send these prophets, but they ran. I did not speak to them, but they prophesied. But if they had stood in my council, then they would have announced My Words to My people, and would have turned them back from their evil way and from the evil of their deeds.

How about this next scripture! Does this not sound like the nightly news?

Jeremiah 25:32 (NASB)—Thus says the Lord of Hosts, "*Behold, evil is going forth from nation to nation* (terrorists in today's world) and **a great whirlwind** is being stirred up from the remotest parts of the earth.

Jeremiah 30:23-24 (NASB)—Behold, **the whirlwind of The Lord!** Wrath has gone forth, **a sweeping tempest;** *it will burst on the head of the*

wicked. The fierce anger of The Lord will not turn back, until He has performed, and until He has accomplished the intent of His heart; in the Latter Days you will understand this.

Ezekiel 1:4-5B, 12, 24-28, 3:16-19 (NASB)—And as I looked, behold, **a whirlwind** was coming forth from the north, <u>**a great cloud with fire flashing forth continually and a bright light around it, and in its midst something like glowing metal in the midst of the fire.**</u> And within it there were figures resembling four living beings. And each went straight forward, wherever the Spirit was about to go, they would go without turning as they went. I also heard the sound of their wings like the sound of abundant waters as they went, like the voice of The Almighty, a sound of tumult like the sound of an army camp; whenever they stood still, they dropped their wings. And there came a voice from above the expanse that was over their heads; whenever they stood still, they dropped their wings. Now above the expanse that was over their heads there was something resembling a throne, like lapis lazuli in appearance; and on that which resembled a throne, high up, was a figure with the appearance of a man. Then I noticed the appearance of His loins and upward something like glowing metal that looked like fire all around within it, and from the appearance of His loins and downward I saw something like fire; and there was a radiance around Him. *As the appearance of the rainbow in the clouds on a rainy day, so was the appearance of the surrounding radiance. Such was the appearance of the likeness of the Glory of The Lord. And when I saw it, I fell on my face and heard a voice speaking,* <u>*"Son of man, I have appointed you a watchman to the house of Israel; whenever you hear a word from My mouth, warn them from Me. When I say to the wicked, 'You shall surely die,' and you do not warn him or speak out to warn the wicked from his wicked way that he may live, that wicked man shall die in his iniquity, but his blood I will require at your hand. Yet if you have warned the wicked, and he does not turn from his wickedness or from his wicked way, he shall die in his iniquity; but you have delivered yourself."*</u> (God's great Love brings us a warning---to warn others in advance)

The Whirlwind of The Lord---an instrument for salvation and deliverance to those who turn their hearts and their ways to Him, or, in opposition, an instrument of God's anger and justice to those who refuse to submit to His just ways and His eternal Word.

<u>Joshua 24:15</u>

And if it seem evil unto you to serve the Lord, ***choose you this day whom you will serve***; whether the gods which your fathers served that were on the other side of the flood, or the gods of the Amorites, in whose land ye dwell: **<u>but as for me and my house, we will serve the Lord.</u>** Amen!!!

DROUGHT AND FAMINE

Several years ago, when our oldest daughter Beth was in college, I went to visit her in her apartment. She graciously let me sleep in her bed and she chose the couch. I slept well that night and woke up much earlier than I figured she would be getting up, so, as I do many times, I lay there praying for my family and friends. As I prayed, I heard a clear word from the Lord when He said, "Read James chapter 5." Well, He had been telling me for quite some time to do that very thing, but every time I set off to read it, I always seemed to get sidetracked by other scriptures on my way to James 5. SO…..I determined that THIS time I was going to be obedient to the voice of the Lord.

I read the entire chapter, but when I got to the end of the chapter, a certain portion of it rang a loud bell in my ears. I'll share what it says with you: James 5:17 (AMP)-- "¹⁷ Elijah was a man with a nature like ours [with the same physical, mental, and spiritual limitations and shortcomings], and **he prayed intensely for it not to rain, and it did not rain on the earth for three years and six months**."

It hit me like a ton of bricks that what I had just read, (and I had read it many times years before without this impact) was a major life and death issue. This scripture was speaking of the land of Israel which is a semi-arid part of the world already! In other words, very little rain fell BEFORE Elijah was told to call a drought on the land, so the results of his prayer could be devastating for the people of Israel. I was baffled!!! Why would You, Lord, Who loves Your People so much, direct one of your prophets to pray such a prayer that could be so devastating?

And pretty quickly I got an answer. He spoke to my heart that He had, in His Mercy and Loving-kindness, told His people over and over and over again through His prophets, to have NOTHING to do with the nations around them; not to marry their sons and daughters, and to keep themselves pure from their idolatrous ways. But His people, in their sin of rebellious pride, had over and over made the deadly decision to ignore His counsel and go their own way. They had done exactly the opposite of what He had warned them through His prophets and as a result SUCH a crop of ungodliness of such enormous proportions had grown up in their land that God had no alternative but to call for drastic measures to destroy that crop, for the sake of His Name and for the future of His people. Gigantic sin called for gigantic measures.

I believe that this is the precipice upon which this once great nation of ours stands today. We have, due to our enormous sin of pride which so loudly and so clearly sounds from our rooftops, said, "It does not matter what God has said in His Word. You do whatever feels good to you and do not worry about the consequences. You only live once so live it up! JUST DO IT!!!" Sounds like a modern day rendition of what Satan (Read about it in Genesis 3), through the words of the cunning serpent in the Garden of Eden said to Adam and Eve, and which brought such negative effects on every person who has ever lived since that infamous day in history.

There seems to be nothing sacred anymore— not purity before marriage, not the sanctity of marriage, not the sanctity of human life, not integrity in government, in business and personal relationships, not Truth. And I believe, as many others do, that the United States of America is headed toward sure destruction if we do not change our minds and turn and go the other way, the way of God's Truth. He allowed our enemies to send this nation a warning on September 11, 2001, which we seemed to heed temporarily when the churches were filled with people asking God for help in our time of greatest need. But sadly, as the dust cleared and we resumed our normal daily activities, we as a nation went back to our old thought patterns and our deadly ways, and here we are again at a crossroad with impending consequences from which we may never recover unless repentance becomes a reality in our hearts and minds. Many people, including many Christians, believe that the word repentance means to turn and go the other way. But in actuality, the Greek word "metanoia" from which it comes, is the word which denotes "a new mindset, to change one's mind about a matter". THEN, once the struggle is won on the battlefield of the mind, the word "epistrepho", which means to turn and go the other way, can kick in. No thought pattern turn-around, no life path turnaround. What can change our minds to that degree? The Word of God and ONLY the Word of God!!!

I believe that there is hope, but only if we recognize the base problem, PRIDE; only if we humble ourselves before God and confess, "O God, we have sinned against You and You alone. We have lifted up our pride-filled hearts and minds and have forgotten You! We have forgotten Your Word upon which this once great nation was founded; Your Word which we once believed as the sure foundation of this great country. O God, have Mercy on us. Forgive us of our great sin, of our pride and all its expressions. We need Your Son Jesus, the ONLY Way, the ONLY Truth and the ONLY Life. Lead us, O God, into Your Path of Life according to Your Spirit. Help us, O Lord, to depend entirely upon You and to take the time to listen to Your Voice which, by Your Love, leads us only to blessing. In Jesus' name we pray. Amen."

So as we read in 1 Kings 17:1 (AMP)-- 17 Now Elijah the Tishbite, who was of the settlers of Gilead, said to Ahab, "As the LORD, the God of Israel lives, before whom I stand, **there shall be neither dew nor rain these years, except by My word**." God did exactly as He had said He would do, out of His great Love for His children who had disobeyed His clear Word to them. And the drought was on. NO RAIN for three and a half years. Can you even imagine that?! A drastic measure to eradicate a drastic rebellion against His Word. A loving parent chastening His beloved children, indeed.

Now read the poignant story of the widow who had to put feet to her faith in 1 Kings 17:8-15 (NASB)--8 Then the word of the LORD came to him, saying, 9 "Arise, go to Zarephath, which belongs to Sidon, and stay there; behold, I have commanded a widow there to provide for you." 10 So he arose and went to Zarephath, and when he came to the gate of the city, behold, a widow was there gathering sticks; and he called to her and said, "Please get me a little water in a jar, that I may drink." 11 As she was going to get *it*, he called to her and said, "Please bring me a piece of bread in your hand." [12] But she said, "As the LORD your God lives, **I have no bread, only a handful of flour in the bowl and a little oil in the jar; and behold, I am gathering a few sticks that I may go in and prepare for me and my son, that we may eat it and die**." [13] **Then Elijah said to her, "Do not fear; go, DO as you have said, but make me a little bread cake from it FIRST,** and bring *it* out to me, and afterward you may make *one* for yourself and for your son. [14] For thus says the LORD God of Israel, '**The bowl of flour shall not be exhausted, nor shall the jar of oil be empty, until the day that the LORD sends rain on the face of the earth**.' [15] **So she went and did according to the word of Elijah, and she and he and her household ate for *many* days**.

What clearer message could He send to let us know that He cares for the down and out, the widow and the orphan, the poor of this world? What Love and Compassion and supernatural Power to provide for His children!!! He wants the best for us. He's willing to minister His "dunamis" (the Greek word for our word dynamite) power to demonstrate His Love to us. But that poor, hopeless widow had to DO something in faith first, something hard to understand. She had to hear the Word of the Lord first, then she had to obey, as discomforting as this Word was. She had to use up what she had left, hers and her son's last morsel of sustenance, to provide food for the prophet first, so that God could show Himself as the incomprehensible Loving God that He is.

Oh, that we would do so today. Oh, that the Church would hear the Word of the Lord as He speaks loudly and clearly to us, asking us to lay down our sinful, worldly ways, our lust for money and power and prestige and things that do not satisfy. He longs for us to come to Him in humility of heart and mind, and to know that He strongly desires to be in Blood Covenant with us. He told us that He will truly supply ALL of our needs according to HIS riches in glory, by Christ Jesus (Philippians 4:13) WHEN we walk and talk together in a love relationship that is beyond words.

God wants the rain of His Spirit to fall on America once again. He is ready, as a Loving Father will always do, to forgive us and to release the showers of blessings upon us, IF we will but come back into His Loving Arms, hear His heartbeat and obey His Word. In James 5:18 (NIV) He speaks these life-giving Words: [18] **"Again he prayed, and the heavens gave rain, and the earth produced its crops."**

America, and every country around the world, we MUST change our mind about the path we are taking. We MUST realize before it's too late that the road we are on is a road which leads only to destruction. Choose Life and do it today! This is our last chance! God's Grace and Mercy have provided us one more opportunity to decide FOR Him......not against Him. Let's ask Him for the rain to fall again on our dry and thirsty lands.

Listen to what God says at the end of the chapter in James 5, [19] "**My brethren, if anyone among you strays from the Truth and falls into error and another person brings him back to God, [20] Let the latter one be sure that <u>whoever turns a sinner from his evil course will save that one's soul from death and will cover a multitude of sins</u> [procure the pardon of the many sins committed by the convert]".** Turn back to God now, before it's too late. He's waiting FOR YOU with His arms open wide.

PULLING WEEDS

When my husband Randy and I moved to our little town in Central Florida we first moved into a two bedroom apartment where we stayed for about a year and a half. We began the search at that point for a little house to purchase, and pretty quickly found one, a total fixer-upper. Thinking back now we should have been on one of those HGTV home improvement shows. What a huge mess it was, even though the house itself was rather small. I spent 8 hours just cleaning all the grease and crud off the stove/oven, so you can only imagine what the rest of the house and yard were like. But we got a great price for it and were excited and happy to own our own home for the first time in our married lives.

We worked and we worked and we worked, digging through the years of "stuff" the former owners had left for us to clean up, until finally, the inside of the house was in pretty good shape. But then, my eyes looked out to the yard. Oh, my!!! Randy had to go off to work each day, and because I had quit my job to stay home and take care of our new house, it was left to me to get the yard in shape. Mission Impossible, it seemed, but I was willing to do whatever it took to get the job done, for as my dear Dad had taught me, hard work never hurt anybody.

I clipped and I bagged and I dug and I pulled weeds until I thought my fingers would fall off. One day, as I was out in the open yard, pulling weeds yet again, the Lord pointed out a valuable lesson to me. Sometimes it is needful for us to pull out some of what we would consider to be the good grass, the things in our lives that WE may have planted or that WE would like to keep because it looks or feels good, along with the weeds in whose root systems the good grass is entangled; the weeds that are choking the life out of us. Then, and only then, can the grass that remains have the necessary room and the sustenance it needs to maintain healthy growth and beautifully cover the landscape of our lives.

"CAN GOD PREPARE A TABLE IN THE WILDERNESS?"

In Psalm 78:14-20 (NASB) God's Word tells us "He led them (the Hebrew nation) with the cloud by day and all the night with light of fire. He split the rocks in the wilderness and gave them abundant drink like the ocean depths. He brought forth streams also from the rock and caused waters to run down like rivers. YET, they still continued to sin against Him, to rebel against the Most High in the desert. And in their heart they put God to the test by asking food according to their desire. **Then they spoke against God. They said, "Can God prepare a table in the wilderness?"**

Let me go back quite a few years. My husband Randy and I waited for exactly 9 years and 1 week to have a baby. Now this was not by our choice after the first few years of marriage had passed, law school had been completed, and Randy was established as an attorney in our hometown. No, definitely not our choice.

As I had mentioned earlier, I engulfed myself daily in scriptures, and spent much time in prayer using the book "Prayers that Avail Much" in which the author had compiled many Bible verses into very life-applicable prayers so that you are actually praying God's Word over the situation or the person about whom you are concerned. I made a practice of hiding God's Word in my heart every day, and little did I know the magnitude of the blessing all that would be later on down the road in our lives, years after God had blessed us with our two precious daughters.

On October 31,1995 (Trick or Treat!!!) I was diagnosed with very aggressive and very advanced breast cancer. We chose to go to a teaching hospital 2-1/2 hours from our home for the major portion of my treatment. I was absolutely terrified of needles at that time, and my poor husband really didn't know if I was going to be able to make it through all the procedures that lay ahead of me after the very first IV they gave me to prepare me for a scan caused me to shake uncontrollably out of sheer fear.

I had found the lump in my breast shortly after I had had a physical which included a clear mammogram---that's how fast it had grown. I should have, I admit, gone to the doctor much earlier than I did, but for the way the lump reacted to caffeine. It would swell up if I drank tea or coffee, or even if I vacuumed the floor. It was very painful and very movable. I just wanted to believe it was a cyst like so many of my friends had experienced AND because of how scared I was to have a needle poked into me. Please, do not make the mistake I made if you detect a lump. I almost waited too long.

Well, I went through two months of aggressive chemotherapy with all its negative side effects, a radical mastectomy, a stem cell transplant using my own stem cells which had been extracted from my blood and frozen to await the transplant after having been given the most powerful dose of chemotherapy a body can tolerate. I almost didn't make it through that one, and then, lastly, 30 radiation treatments. Eight long months of treatment, most of it away from my husband who was trying to maintain his law office practice and take care of our 6 year old and 9 year old daughters and our home. He was amazing!!!

In the beginning there was such dismay and unbelief, then thoughts of wanting to escape, then raw anger. I told God in no uncertain terms with a finger pointed toward Heaven that He didn't care what was happening to me, that He had forgotten me and had left my universe. A week and a half later, as I sat in the back of our church, away from everyone due to my compromised immune system as a result of chemotherapy, The Lord spoke to my heart and reminded me that all those people I was looking at, and so many more who had prayed for me and my family, had called to get updates, had sent cards and letters to encourage me, had cooked and brought food to my family, had babysat our little girls, had driven me long distances for treatment, and our long time friends Linda and Angie who had cleaned our house when we couldn't do so, were all a part of God's Plan to care for and provide for me, Randy and the girls. "Wow! I am so sorry, Lord. Please forgive me".

We had dear friends, the Reid family, right there in the city where I was receiving treatment. A few years prior to this time, God had so "uncaringly" moved them away from our hometown, but they, it turned out, had actually been so lovingly placed by His loving hands to be exactly where we needed them most to care for me when Randy couldn't be there to do so. They gave so sacrificially, it was as if they were God's heart, His hands, His feet and mouthpiece to me, Randy and the girls. I met people I would never have met in my entire life who ministered to me there, and to whom I pray I was also a minister of God's Love.

We were going through the toughest trial of our entire lives, but do you know what? All those scriptures I had set to memory all those years before as we had believed God for a child were coming back to me, just when we needed them most. My dear friend Doreen, told me that she had never seen anyone like me (and all praise to God for this!) because God's Word would just flow out of my mouth like rivers of living water, which was an encouragement to all those around me and to me in the midst of this enormous storm. The living Power of the Word----there is NOTHING like it!!! NOTHING!!!

God spoke so clearly to me through a scripture that came off the pages of the Bible to me during this turbulent time, and that was Jeremiah 15:15-21 (KJV):

"Thou Who knowest, O Lord, remember me. Take notice of me, and take vengeance for me on my persecutors (those vile cancer cells). Do not, in view of Thy patience, take me away. Know that for Thy sake I endure reproach. Thy Words were found and I did eat them, and Thy Words became for me the joy and rejoicing of my heart. For I have been called by Thy name, O Lord God of Hosts. Why has my pain been perpetual, and my wound incurable, refusing to be healed? Wilt Thou indeed be to me like a deceptive stream with water that is unreliable? Therefore, says the Lord, 'If you return then I will restore you---before Me you will stand. And if you extract the precious from the worthless, you will become my spokesman." "Hey, wait just a minute, God. Not me. No way!!!" "Yes Way," He answered me in my stubbornness and less than humble response to Him.

So…I started witnessing to my doctors and nurses, and other patients. Now you need to understand that up to that point I had been one of the shyest people on the planet. I started declaring Proverbs 28:1 (AMP) which says, "The righteous are as bold as a lion," because it was not in me to be bold, that's for sure!!! I started leaving Gospel tracts at the hospital, in stores and restaurants, everywhere I went to spread the good news that God is Love! God changed me from the inside out right in the middle of a life crisis. Only He can do that, and He did, and is still in the process every day.

When all my treatment was finally over, I told many of my friends and family, "I would never want to go through that again, but I wouldn't have traded that experience for anything in the world." The Lord has given me so many opportunities to speak to individuals and to groups as a result of what we went through, and I know that I have an army of Christian friends and family who did, and still do, pray for me and lift me up on a regular basis. I have said so many times, "I DO NOT KNOW HOW ANYONE CAN GO THROUGH A TRIAL LIKE THIS WITHOUT THE LORD AND WITHOUT CHRISTIAN FRIENDS AND FAMILY TO HOLD THEM UP!!!" I am so very thankful for every person who blessed me and my family through that incredibly hard time in our lives. You all were and are truly a gift from God.

So the rest of the prophecy that I like to say Jeremiah wrote "just for me" goes like this in verses 20 and 21: "For I am with you to save you and deliver you," declares the Lord. "So I will deliver you from the hand of the wicked, and I will redeem you from the grasp of the violent." And He did, and I thank Him with all of my heart.

Now the real answer to the question with which we began this chapter, "Can God prepare a table in the wilderness?" is so wonderfully answered in a verse that has blessed so many through the centuries, and that is Psalm 23:5-6 (NIV)—**"You prepare a table before me in the presence of my enemies**. You anoint my head with oil; my cup overflows. ⁶ Surely your goodness and love will follow me all the days of my life, and I will dwell in the house of the LORD forever." He did it for me. Let Him do it for you.

A STORY OF GRACE

A few years ago I drove down to work on our two condos which we rent in the Boca Grande area on the west coast of Florida. As some of my friends and family well know, I love doing home improvement projects. I've always said, "I don't care how hard the work or how messy the project, when I get a vision for how something is going to look when it's done, I'm on it 'til it's finished!!!" It's truly a passion of mine.

Well, I had had a bee in my bonnet for 11 years about one of our condo's back porches. When the building was originally constructed, they did a "not so great" painting job on the walls of the screened lanai. It wasn't horrible, but it was just bad enough that it bugged me every time I was there. I bought decorative items to hang on the walls to try to camouflage the problem, but I still saw the problem as if it was lit up with neon lights every time I saw it. My dear husband had told me not to worry about it, but that was not going to happen. SOOOO....down I went, finally, with painting supplies in hand. And up I went on the ladder to trim out the 10 foot ceiling line and all the vertical lines bordering the screen frames and rather large sliding glass doors. The condo association supplied the paint which was a very different shade than the original paint, but as it dried I came to think I'd like it.

And suddenly, it was finished!!! The walls looked so fresh and clean (it's always so amazing what a can of paint can do to change the feeling in a room)! I loved it!!! BUT, now the concrete floors that had been painted to look like large ceramic tiles with their fake grout lines looked terrible. That floor had been my nemesis for all those years with its very rough surface that caught every particle of dirt that blew by! No matter how many gallons of hot soapy water I carried from the kitchen to the back porch, and no matter how hard I scrubbed, it always looked dirty. AAARRRGGGHHH!!! What to do? I hadn't planned on THIS project!!! Nothing to do but run down to the local hardware store, one of my favorite places in the whole world to visit in order to make dreams come true, and inquired of the behind-the-counter-paint-man how to go about this challenge. I first asked him if he had ½" painters tape to seal off the grout lines, and he promptly told me no. Oh, wow!!! I hadn't thought past that issue, just knowing that they would have what I needed. Well, I got the patio floor paint color I thought would match the original color, and the grout line paint color all mixed, then felt led to buy the smallest paint brush they had hanging amongst the large assortment of brushes. I got the roller he suggested after I told him it was a pretty rough surface, but it turned out that the roller was much too smooth for this application, giving me quite the upper body workout I had not expected once I got into the project.

Well, that floor was a total paint sucker, and I could tell rather quickly that one gallon was not going to do it, so quick change into my street clothes from my well decorated paint clothes, and back to the hardware store to purchase another gallon. I definitely should have gotten a different roller at that point but didn't want to go through the mess of changing rollers. Big mistake!

Got the whole floor covered, or so I thought. Now the entire time I had painted, the autumn southern sun was blasting the whole area making it extremely difficult to tell what had been covered well and what had not, since I had picked a very similar color to the original paint color. I let it dry and then excitedly walked around to see the progress I had made. NOT!!! Another coat was absolutely necessary, so out came the inadequate roller once again and another workout ensued. "Oh well, it's so worth it", I thought.

Next day, I sat on the floor in the sunshine with my little paint brush and bucket of paint and meticulously hand painted the fake grout lines. This actually turned out to be quite relaxing and fun as I could paint all the lines around me, look up and enjoy the incredible waterview from the porch, then move my supplies and continue my satisfying work. It looked like a brand new porch….UNTIL I carefully inspected the floor after it dried and realized, as I cast my shadow across any part of it, that the tiny black pits that had been hidden by the brilliant sunshine each time I had painted the main floor were still there! I could not use the roller due to the fact that I had already painted my grout lines and sure wasn't going to do that again, no matter how much fun it had been. Goodness!!! Are you feeling my frustration? I sure was! Would I EVER get this back porch finished? I was beginning to doubt it but was even more determined that I was in it for the long haul now.

Out came the big brush and paint bucket, as I "pushed" the paint down into those little holes, thinking that I was actually making progress as I completed each square. But alas and alack!!! When all that dried, and as I did my walk-through inspection, I realized once again that my shadow was revealing all the pits that had once again been hidden by the bright sunlight!!! At that point, as I sat and hand painted it AGAIN, I asked the Lord, "What are you trying to show me through this exercise in self-control, patience and determination, dear God?"

It was as if He said to me, "I'm SO glad you asked!" And then it came, something so profound, something I would never have thought of in a million years through the administration of two gallons of paint. There are instances in which we or someone dear to us who have been raised in the bright light of the Word of God have, for whatever reason, turned away from that Truth and fallen into dark pits of various kinds. But God, through His awesome Love and sovereignty, can use what the enemy meant for evil, through our prayers of intercession, to turn us, or them, back to The Way, The Truth and The Life that comes only through believing in and following His Son Jesus Christ. And when that occurs, He can use our knowledge of that dark place, the shadow in which we've lived, to expose those pits of darkness in other's lives, empathize with them, and help them in a way that only those who have been there and done that can do.

The shadows we cast become light for those in darkness. It's kind of crazy but I've seen it happen in so many lives.. This so reminded me of the times, as I mentioned in an earlier chapter, in which I had sat there listening to talk after talk during the women's ministry weekends. I heard from their own mouths stories of people who had been to the brink of destruction due to their own poor choices, or in some instances others' poor choices for them, to walk in darkness. There was seemingly no hope for their future. But then one day, in a moment of time, they came to themselves, and walked out of that darkness and into Light because someone who had experienced that same darkness beforehand had testified to the Grace of God and had made the decision to earnestly pray for their deliverance until it became a reality (The Fortress).

In Genesis 50:20 (AMP), Joseph said to his brothers (who had first planned to kill him then decided to sell him to a group of nomads due to their intense jealousy and hatred caused by his incessant boasting about the dreams and visions God had given him), "²⁰ **As for you, you thought evil against me, but God meant it for good, to bring about that many people should be kept alive, as they are this day.**" Now THAT'S what I'm talking about!!!

Let 's decide today that no matter where we've been, no matter what we've done, no matter whom we've hurt or who has hurt us, that God's Grace overcomes it all. God's Grace—blessing us even when we don't deserve it in ways only He can use to be a blessing to us, and then to others in our journey.

AH, THEM BONES!

I have always been fascinated with the scriptures revealed to the prophet Ezekiel that tell the story of the resurrection of the nation of Israel in Ezekiel 37 (AMP). I can so easily see the words of the prophet coming to life, in obedience to the Power-filled Word of the Lord to His People. Take a few minutes to read the account in the Amplified version:

1 The hand of the LORD was upon me, and He brought me out in the Spirit of the LORD and set me down **in the middle of the valley; and it was full of bones**. ²He caused me to pass all around them, and behold, *there were* **very many [human bones] in the open valley**; and lo, *they were* **very dry**. ³And He said to me, "**Son of man, can these bones live?**" And I answered, "O Lord GOD, You know."

⁴Again He said to me, "**Prophesy** (speak forth My Word) **to these bones** and say to them, 'O dry bones, <u>**hear the word of the LORD**</u>.' ⁵Thus says the Lord GOD to these bones, <u>**'Behold, I will make breath enter you so that you may come to life**</u>. ⁶I will put sinews on you, make flesh grow back on you, cover you with skin, and I will put breath in you so that you may come alive; and **you will know that I am the LORD.**'"

⁷So I prophesied as I was commanded; and as I prophesied, **there was a [thundering] noise, and behold, a rattling** (the Whirlwind); and the bones came together, bone to its bone. ⁸And I looked, and behold, there were sinews on the bones, and flesh grew and skin covered them; but there was no breath in them. ⁹Then He said to me, "**Prophesy to the breath**, son of man, and say to the breath, 'Thus says the Lord GOD, "**Come from the four winds**, O breath, and breathe on these slain, **that they may live**." ¹⁰So I prophesied as He commanded me, and <u>**the breath came into them, and they came to life and stood up on their feet**</u>, an exceedingly great army.

The Vision Explained

¹¹ Then He said to me, "Son of man, these bones are the whole house of Israel. Behold, they say, 'Our bones are dried up and our hope is lost. We are completely cut off.' ¹² Therefore prophesy and say to them, 'Thus says the Lord God, "Behold, I will open your graves and make you come up out of your graves, My people; and I will bring you [back home] to the land of Israel. ¹³ **Then you will know [with confidence] that I am the Lord, when I have opened your graves and made you come up out of your graves, My people. ¹⁴ I will put My Spirit in you and you will come to life,** and I will place you in your own land. Then you will know that I the Lord have spoken, and fulfilled it," says the Lord.'

²⁶ **I will make a covenant of peace with them**; it shall be an everlasting covenant with them, and I will give blessings to them and multiply them and will set My sanctuary in the midst of them forevermore. ²⁷ **My tabernacle,** *My* **dwelling place also shall be with them; and I WILL BE THEIR GOD, THEY SHALL BE MY PEOPLE.**

What a God! What a loving Father! To take people who have no hope, no matter who they are and no matter what they've done, and breathe new life into their lifeless bodies and souls.

Now look at the following verses that speak to OUR bodily and mental health and our bones.

PROVERBS 3:5-9 (MSG)--**Trust God from the bottom of your heart**; don't try to figure out everything on your own. Listen for God's voice in everything you do, everywhere you go; he's the one who will keep you on track. Don't assume that you know it all. Run to God! Run from evil! **Your body will glow with health, your very bones will vibrate with life**! Honor God with everything you own; give him the first and the best.

ISAIAH 58:9-12—(God's Word Translation-GW)--⁹ Then you will call, and the Lord will answer. You will cry for help, and he will say, "Here I am!" Get rid of that yoke. Don't point your finger and say wicked things. ¹⁰ **If you give some of your own food to** feed **those who are hungry and**

to satisfy the needs of **those who are humble, then your light will rise in the dark, and your darkness will become as bright as the noonday sun.** [11] The LORD will continually guide you and satisfy you even in sun-baked places. **He will strengthen your bones.** You will become like a watered garden and like a spring whose water does not stop flowing. [12] Your people will rebuild the ancient ruins and restore the foundations of past generations. You will be called the Rebuilder of Broken Walls and the Restorer of Streets Where People Live.

See what only God can do with your life:

Psalm 51:7-8 (MSG)--Soak me in your laundry and I'll come out clean, scrub me and I'll have a snow-white life. Tune me in to foot-tapping songs, **set these once-broken bones to dancing**.

See what can happen when our thoughts and emotions are positive, but also when they're not:

Proverbs 14:30 (MSG)--**A sound mind makes for a robust body**, but **runaway emotions corrode the bones**.

SEE what God sees!!! SPEAK what God speaks!!! Study His Word and hide It in your hearts to show yourselves approved, workmen who do not need to be ashamed, but who rightly divide the Word of Truth. (2 Timothy 2:15-KJV). THEN, you will come to KNOW, TO UNDERSTAND, AND TO REALIZE THAT HE IS THE SOVEREIGN LORD, AND THAT HE HAS PERFORMED WHAT HE SAID HE WOULD DO (Jeremiah 1:12—AMP), just as He did for a people who had given up all hope, but whom God caused to rise up to new life again, for His Glory, for His Honor and for their good.

CAN YOU SEE IT, MY BROTHER AND SISTER?
HOPE IN THE LORD ALWAYS! HE ALONE
CAN RAISE YOU UP FROM DEATH TO LIFE! TAKE
THAT FIRST STEP TOWARD YOUR LOVING HEAVENLY
FATHER AND HE'LL COME RUNNING!!!

DADS AGAINST THE DEVIL

Once as I was praying back in May of 1998, I saw a vision of the president of the United States in his oval office. Now it was quickly brought to my attention that the president was in this picture simply because he held the highest ranking position in the world. As he sat at his desk, he quickly picked up the red phone, the hot line, as it rang, bringing him the dreaded message that an enemy nuclear missile was headed directly toward the United States, a missile capable of killing or injuring most of the inhabitants of our country. He immediately grabbed the phone next to the hot line and spoke the words no president ever wants to speak, "Incoming, set your aim and fire!" The unnamed man at the other end, with his vast array of advanced detector devices, pinpointed the missile, pressed the red button and fired a missile that was equipped with the technology and power to seek, find, and destroy the fast approaching weapon of mass destruction. American citizens, unaware of the thwarted plan of the enemy to annihilate us, went on as usual, feeling very safe and secure in our everyday activities.

I asked the Lord what the vision meant. He showed me that the source of the initial intelligence report is God Himself, who is always ready to help us defeat the enemy at a moment's notice, IF we are alert and watching, as He has told us to be and to do. The president represents the Holy Spirit who lives within the hearts of those who have elected to have Him there "in office". The unnamed man in the picture is symbolic of all the fathers, the dads who have been appointed by God to be the watchmen on the wall for their wives and sons and daughters, the widows and the orphans. Now that anonymous man in the picture could have been away from his post, busy and distracted by other things, or just unconcerned and not available to pick up the phone, missing the vital communication from the top. In that case, United States citizens would have been blown off the planet with no warning. However, the man had over the years chosen to wholeheartedly be on the alert, to study the manual, and to be trained by others skilled in warfare and technology so that when the need arose he was totally prepared for the attack without a blink of the eye. No doubt, no indecision, no fear pervaded his thoughts. He knew he had heard from the top ranking authority and he was ready to carry out his duty on behalf of those under his care. When the president spoke, the proper action was taken and the lives of millions were saved.

I believe it is absolutely crucial that in what may be the last days of life as we have known it before the coming of the Lord, the dads of our nation must all individually and as a body of Godly men be willing and ready to prepare themselves to meet the challenge Satan throws up against them and their families. Most of you are no doubt already familiar with the power of the whole armor of God and the Blood of Jesus with which you need to daily cover yourself and your families. We all know, or need to know, about the power in knowing and teaching the names of God and their infinite meaning to our families, and the power of the Holy Spirit. But how many fathers are taking the time to turn off whatever activity holds their attention and meditate on God's Word day and night, hiding it deeply within their hearts so that we and our families will have good success, and not be taken by surprise when the enemy sends his weapons of destruction?

An Old Testament chapter caught my attention several years ago in relation to this important subject. It's I Kings 20:1-14, 22-30 (AMP)--1**Ben-hadad king of Aram (Syria) gathered all his army together;** thirty-two kings were [allied] with him, with horses and chariots. And he went up and besieged Samaria [Israel's capital], and fought against it. ² Then he sent messengers to the city to Ahab king of Israel; and he said to him, **"Thus says Ben-hadad:** ³ **'Your silver and your gold are mine; your wives and your children, even the fairest, also are mine [as conditions of peace].'"** ⁴ **The king of Israel [conceded his defeat and] answered, "By your word, my lord, O king, I am yours, and all that I have**." (Dads, we CANNOT let this be said of us and our families!!!) ⁵ The messengers returned and said, "Thus says Ben-hadad: 'I indeed sent *word* to you, saying, "You shall give me your silver, your gold, your wives, and your children," ⁶ **but about this time tomorrow I will send my servants to you, and they will search your house and the houses of your servants; and they will take with their hands (confiscate) whatever is desirable in your eyes and carry it away.'"**

⁷ Then the king of Israel summoned all the elders of the land and said, "Please observe and see how this man is seeking our destruction. **For he sent *messengers* to me for my wives, my children, my silver, and my gold, and I did not refuse him**." ⁸ **All the elders and all the people said to him, "Do not listen or consent [to this additional demand]."** ⁹ So he said to Ben-hadad's messengers, "Tell my lord the king, 'Every *demand* you first sent to your servant I will do, **but I cannot do this [additional] thing [as a condition of peace].'"** And the messengers left; then they brought him word again. ¹⁰ Ben-hadad sent *word* to him and said, "May the gods do so to me, and more also, if there is enough dust left of Samaria for handfuls for all the [armed] people who follow me." ¹¹ The king of Israel answered, "Tell him, 'A man who puts on [his armor to go to battle] should not boast like the man who takes it off [after the battle has been won].'" ¹² **When Ben-hadad heard this message, as he and the kings were drinking in the temporary shelters, he said to his servants, "Station *yourselves*."** So they stationed *themselves* against the city [of Samaria].

¹³ **Then a prophet approached Ahab king of Israel and said, "Thus says the Lord: 'Have you seen all this great army? Behold, I will hand them over to you, and you shall know [without any doubt] that I am the Lord.'"** ¹⁴ Ahab said, "By whom?" And he said, "Thus says the Lord: **'By the young men [the attendants or bodyguards] of the governors of the districts.'"** Then Ahab said, "Who shall begin the battle?"

And he answered, "You."

²² **Then the prophet approached the king of Israel and said to him, "Go, strengthen yourself and observe and see what you have to do; for at the first of next year the king of Aram (Syria) will come up against you."** (God warned them well in advance of the coming attack and they were listening!)

²³ **Now the servants of the king of Aram said to him, "Israel's god is a god of the hills; that is why they were stronger than we. But let us fight against them in the plain, and surely we will be stronger than they.** ²⁴ Do this: remove the [thirty-two allied] kings, each from his place, and put captains in their place, ²⁵ and assemble an army like the army that you have lost *in battle*, horse for horse and chariot for chariot. Then we will fight against them in the plain, and surely we shall be stronger than they." And he listened to their words and did so.

²⁶ **At the first of the year [in spring]** (just as the prophet had foretold), **Ben-hadad assembled** *and* counted the Arameans (Syrians) and went up to Aphek [east of the Sea of Galilee] to fight against Israel. ²⁷ The sons of Israel were counted and given provisions, and they went to meet them. **The Israelites camped before the enemy like two little flocks of goats [with everything against them, except God], and the Arameans filled the country.** ²⁸ **A man of God approached and said to the king of Israel, "Thus says the LORD, 'Because the Arameans have said, "The LORD is a god of the hills, but He is not a god of the valleys," <u>I will give this great army into your hand, and you shall know [by experience] that I am the LORD.</u>'"** ²⁹ **So they camped opposite each other for seven days. Then on the seventh day the battle began, and the sons of Israel killed 100,000 of the Aramean foot soldiers in a single day.** ³⁰ **But the rest ran to the city of Aphek, and the [city] wall fell on 27,000 of the men who were left.**

I LOVE IT!!!!!! Yes, Ahab had made huge errors in judgment in the past! In other words, he blew it more than once when it came to taking care of his family and his kingdom, but God's Word says in Proverbs 21:1 (AMP) "The king's heart is like channels of water in the hand of the Lord; He turns it whichever way He wishes." God can redeem the mistakes we've made as parents. He can restore what the canker worm and the locust have eaten (Read Joel 2). He can change the inheritance we've thus far passed down to our descendants, and give our kids and their kids a glorious inheritance for all time, based on God's Word and the faith of our fathers, as evidenced by their actions!!!

I saw in the vision the dads who are ready, in season and out, with the missiles of Almighty God, ready to blast Satan's arrows and missiles off the planet! Picture this:

(1) Satan sends a missile of eternal death to your family. You, dad, send back the missile, "**I believe on the Lord Jesus Christ and I shall be saved <u>and my household</u>.**" (Acts 16:31). BOOM!!!

(2) Satan fires a missile of sickness and disease at you or someone you love. Dad, blast him with, "**God sent His Word to heal us and to deliver us from <u>all</u> our destructions.**" (Psalm 107:20). BOOM!!!

(3) Satan sends a weapon of lukewarmness toward the things of God. You, ready as ever, send up the missile of the prophet Jeremiah who said, "**But if I say, 'I will not remember God or speak anymore in His name, <u>then in my heart it becomes like a burning fire shut up in my bones</u>, and I am weary of holding it in.**" (Jeremiah 20:9). BOOM!!!

(4) When Satan pushes his button to make one of our family members feel like a lowly, insignificant, useless worm, let him have it with, "**<u>Even when we were dead in our sins</u>, God made us alive together with Christ, and <u>seated us with Him in heavenly places in Christ Jesus</u>!**" (Ephesians 2:5-6) Hallelujah!!! TAKE THAT, you old serpent!!!

(5) And when we or our family members feel that we have gone too far, and have sinned too greatly, stick it to the devil with, "**<u>As far as the east is from the west</u>, so far has He removed our transgressions from us.**" (Psalm 103:12). BOOM!!!

(6) When that slimy dragon tries to perpetuate a curse down through the generations, knock his lights out with, "**<u>Christ redeemed us from the curse of the law</u>, having become a curse for us,**" (Galatians 3:13), and "**<u>The Lord Himself has cut in two the cords of the wicked</u>!**" (Psalm 129:4) KABOOM!!!

(7) When Satan makes you or your loved ones feel all alone, dejected and rejected, cut him down in mid-air with "Jesus said, '**I will never leave you nor forsake you**," and "He **always lives to make intercession for us.**" (Hebrews 13:5) and (Hebrews 7:25) KABLOOWEY!!!

Consider this from Proverbs 24:10-14 (MSG) --[10] "**If you fall to pieces in a crisis, there wasn't much to you in the first place.** [11-12] Rescue the perishing; don't hesitate to step in and help. If you say, 'Hey, that's none of my business,' will that get you off the hook? Someone is watching you closely, you know**—Someone not impressed with weak excuses. [13-14] Eat honey, dear child—it's good for you—and delicacies that melt in your mouth. **Likewise knowledge, and wisdom for your soul—Get that and your future's secured, your hope is on solid rock**."

And this from Psalm 18:30-42, and 18:46-50 (MSG)--[30] What a God! His road stretches straight and smooth. Every GOD-direction is road-tested. **Everyone who runs toward him makes it**. [31-42] **Is there any god like GOD?** Are we not at bedrock? **Is not this the God who armed me, then aimed me in the right direction.** Now I run like a deer; I'm king of the mountain. He shows me how to fight; I can bend a bronze bow! **You protect me with salvation-armor**; you hold me up with a firm hand, caress me with your gentle ways. You cleared the ground under me so my footing was firm. When I chased my enemies I caught them; I nailed them; they were down for good.. You armed me well for this fight, you smashed the upstarts. You made my enemies turn tail.. They cried "uncle" but Uncle didn't come; they yelled for GOD and got no for an answer. They gusted in the wind. I threw them out, like garbage in the gutter.

[46-48] **Live, GOD! Blessings from my Rock, my free and freeing God, towering! This God set things right for me** and shut up the people who talked back. He rescued me from enemy anger, He pulled me from the grip of upstarts, He saved me from the bullies. [49-50] That's why I'm thanking You, GOD, all over the world. That's why I'm singing songs that rhyme Your name. God's king takes the trophy; **God's chosen is beloved, all his children—always**.

God has already revealed and freely given us all we need to live Godly lives. "BELIEVE ON THE LORD JESUS CHRIST AND YOU WILL BE SAVED, AND YOUR HOUSEHOLD!!!" "FOR I HAVE GIVEN YOU EVERYTHING PERTAINING TO LIFE AND GODLINESS!!!" He says. Our families are on the firing line, don't you see? Our country is at the bargaining table. Will we give up and give our children and country over to the enemy of our souls or will we make the choice to serve the Lord, as well-trained soldiers in the most prestigious army that has ever been assembled, the Army of the Most High God. He is the King of kings and Lord of lords. Jesus has said in Luke 10:19 (RSV), "[19] **Behold, I have given you authority** to tread upon serpents and scorpions (demonic forces), and **over all the power of the enemy; and nothing shall hurt you**!" True belief takes God's Wisdom and effective action. Effective action takes determination, and determination brings victory when we are in God's invincible army. Jeremiah said in Jeremiah 20:11 (NASB), "**But the Lord is with me like a dread champion, therefore my persecutors will stumble and NOT prevail!**" Praise God, our super hero!!!

D.A.D.S.

DEFEATING

ALL THE

DEVIL'S

SCHEMES

DIVINE INHERITANCE

Over all the years of my life I have seen how, in the natural, men and women have passed on to their children and to others whom they love a gift, an inheritance of the good things they desire to be a part of their loved ones' lives. Webster's Dictionary defines inheritance as: "money, property, etc., that is received from someone when that person dies; something from the past that is still important or valuable; the act of inheriting something; the reception of genetic qualities by transmission from parent to offspring; the acquisition of a possession, condition, or trait from past generations".

As I researched this very powerful concept in God's Word, I was amazed at how many times the word "inheritance," or different forms of the word, appear in the Bible. It is obviously, as indicated by the sheer number of its mention, very important to God.

Inheritance coming down through our natural family lines, whether it be good, a blessing, or evil, a curse, affects the lives of every single person on the earth. There is just no way around it. So it is up to us who are here now on the earth to be sure to the utmost degree that the inheritance we pass down to generations to come is one of a sure hope, a guarantee of good things to come. In James 1:17 (AMP) it states that "¹⁷ **Every good thing given and every perfect gift is from above; it comes down from the Father of lights (the Creator and Sustainer of the heavens),** in Whom there is no variation (no rising or setting) or shadow cast by His turning (for He is perfect and never changes)."

See for yourself, through just a portion of many scriptures, the vivid picture of the life-giving thread that winds its way through God's Word concerning this extremely vital matter of inheritance. This cord which is such a huge part of the Blood Covenant He established through His only

Son Jesus as a precious gift to those of us who have chosen, or will choose, due to the indisputable evidence given, Him as Lord and Savior.

1 Samuel 2:8 (NIV) He raises **the poor** from the dust and lifts **the needy** from the ash heap; he seats them with princes and has them **inherit a throne of honor**.

The Lord <u>loves</u> and <u>cares</u> about the poor and needy. His Plan is to lift them up to new life in Him. Who of us has not been poor and needy in some way, helpless to rise up from the dust and hopeless despair of life? But take hope, weary traveler:

Psalm 37:9 (AMP) Those who do evil will be cut off, BUT those who wait for the LORD, they will **inherit the land.** Praise God!!!

I Kings 8:33-36 (NIV) [33] "When your people have been defeated by an enemy because they have sinned against you, and when they turn back to you and give praise to your name, praying and making supplication to you in this temple, [34] then hear from heaven and forgive the sin of your people and bring them back to the land you gave to their ancestors. [35] "When the heavens are shut up and there is no rain because your people have sinned against you (remember Drought and Famine?), and when they pray toward this place and give praise to your name and turn from their sin because you have afflicted them, [36] then hear from heaven and forgive the sin of your servants, your people. Teach them the right way to live, and send rain on the land you gave your people for an **inheritance.**

This is such awesome stuff, but beware!!!

Proverbs 28:10 (AMP) He who leads the upright astray on an evil path will himself fall into his own pit, but the blameless will **inherit** good.

Proverbs 3:35 (AMP) The wise will **inherit** honor *and* glory, but dishonor *and* shame is conferred on fools.

Ephesians 5:5 (AMP) [5] For be sure of this: no immoral, impure, or greedy person—for that one is [in effect] an idolater—has any **inheritance** in the kingdom of Christ and God [for such a person places a higher value on something other than God].

Revelation 21:8 (AMP) [8] But as for the cowards and unbelieving and abominable [who are devoid of character and personal integrity and practice or tolerate immorality], and murderers, and sorcerers [with intoxicating drugs], and idolaters *and* occultists [who practice and teach false religions], and all the liars [who knowingly deceive and twist truth], **their part** (inheritance) will be in the lake that blazes with fire and brimstone, which is the second death."

This is such serious business! We can no longer go on ignoring God's Word and think we'll get away with it, either now or in the future of eternity.

"But praise God! There's such hope in Him because "He is not willing that ANY should perish, but that ALL should come to repentance" (2 Peter 3:9), and "by His kindness He brings them to repentance." (Romans 2:4)

Just take in this compelling story of the jailer who was responsible for holding Paul and Silas in prison for preaching the Good News of Jesus Christ.

Acts 16:30-32 (AMP) [30] and after he brought them out [of the inner prison], he said, "Sirs, what must I do to be saved?" [31] And they answered, "Believe in the Lord Jesus [as your personal Savior and entrust yourself to Him] and you will be saved, you and your household [if they also believe]." [32] And they spoke the word of the Lord [concerning eternal salvation through faith in Christ] to him and to all who were in his house.

Proverbs 13:22 (AMP) A good man leaves an **inheritance** to his children's children, and the wealth of the sinner is stored up for [the hands of] the righteous.

Let's look more in depth into the Blessings God has planned to give His Kids.

Ezekiel 44:28 (AMP) [28] "It [their ministry to Me] shall be as an **inheritance** to them, **for I am their inheritance**." (This is a Blood Covenant term, and how awesome is that!!!)

Matthew 5:5 (AMP) ⁵ "Blessed [inwardly peaceful, spiritually secure, worthy of respect] are the gentle [the kind-hearted, the sweet-spirited, the self-controlled], for they will **inherit** the earth.

Such great news!!! Take it all in!!! God loves YOU!!! THAT'S what He's talking about: His Love for you, _____. Put your name in there!!!

Luke 10:25-28 (AMP) ²⁵ And a certain lawyer [an expert in Mosaic Law] stood up to test Him, saying, "Teacher, what must I do to **inherit** eternal life?" ²⁶ Jesus said to him, "What is written in the Law? How do you read it?" ²⁷ And he replied, "YOU SHALL LOVE THE LORD YOUR GOD WITH ALL YOUR HEART, AND WITH ALL YOUR SOUL, AND WITH ALL YOUR STRENGTH, AND WITH ALL YOUR MIND; AND YOUR NEIGHBOR AS YOURSELF." ²⁸ Jesus said to him, "You have answered correctly; DO THIS *habitually* AND YOU WILL LIVE."

My friend, you are not alone. You are not abandoned or left an orphan. You can be a beloved Child of the most high God TODAY!!!

Romans 4:16 (AMP) ¹⁶ Therefore, [**inheriting**] the promise depends entirely on faith [that is, confident trust in the unseen God], in order that *it may be given* as an act of grace [His unmerited favor and mercy], so that the promise will be [legally] guaranteed to all the descendants [of Abraham]—not only for those [Jewish believers] who keep the Law, but also for those [Gentile believers] who share the faith of Abraham, who is the [spiritual] father of us all.

That means everybody can be in God's Family!!! It's your choice!

Romans 8:17 (AMP) ¹⁷ **And if [we are His] children, [then we are His] heirs also: heirs of God and fellow heirs with Christ [sharing His spiritual blessing and inheritance]**, if indeed we share in His suffering so that we may also share in His glory.

Praise God Almighty!!!! This is so incredible!!! It is such amazing Grace!!!

Galatians 3:22 (AMPC)--But the Scriptures picture all mankind as sinners shut up *and* imprisoned by sin (remember The Fortress?), **so that the inheritance, blessing, which was promised through faith in** Jesus Christ (the Messiah) **might be given** (released, delivered, and committed) **to ALL those who believe, who adhere to and trust in and rely on Him.**

Galatians 3:12-14 (TLB) [12] How different from this way of faith is the way of law, which says that a man is saved by obeying every law of God, without one slip. [13] **But Christ has bought us out from under the doom of that impossible system by taking the curse for our wrongdoing upon Himself (Jesus).** For it is written in the Scripture, "Anyone who is hanged on a tree is cursed" (as Jesus was hung upon a wooden cross). [14] Now God can bless the Gentiles, too, with this same blessing he promised to Abraham; and ALL of us as Christians can have the promised Holy Spirit through this faith.

HALLELUJAH!!!

Ephesians 1:13-14 (AMP) [13] In Him you also who have heard the Word of Truth, the glad tidings (Gospel) of your salvation, and have believed in *and* adhered to *and* relied on Him, were stamped with the seal of the long-promised Holy Spirit. [14] That Spirit is the guarantee of our **inheritance**, the firstfruits, the pledge and foretaste, the down payment on our **heritage,** in anticipation of its full redemption *and* our acquiring complete possession of it (Big Day at the Park)—to the praise of His glory.

Ephesians 1:17(AMPC) [17] For I always pray to the God of our Lord Jesus Christ, the Father of glory, that He may grant you a spirit of wisdom and revelation of insight into mysteries and secrets in the deep and intimate knowledge of Him, [18] by having the eyes of your heart flooded with light (the Fortress), so that you can know *and* understand the hope to which He has called you, and how rich is His glorious **inheritance** in the saints (His set-apart ones).

Colossians 1:12 (AMPC)--Giving thanks to the Father, Who has qualified *and* made us fit to share (through the Blood of His Son Jesus) the portion which is the **inheritance** of the saints (God's holy people) in the Light.

Colossians 3:24 (AMPC) Knowing with all certainty that it is from the Lord and not from men that you will receive the **inheritance which is your real reward.** The One Whom you are actually serving is the Lord Christ (the Messiah).

Praise God! Where else could you possibly go to receive such incredible Blessings!!? NOWHERE!!!

I Peter 1:3-5 (AMPC) ³ Praised (honored, blessed) be the God and Father of our Lord Jesus Christ (the Messiah)! By His boundless mercy we have been born again to an ever-living hope through the resurrection of Jesus Christ from the dead, ⁴ Born anew into an **inheritance** which is beyond the reach of change *and* decay, imperishable, unsullied and unfading, reserved in heaven for you, ⁵ Who are being guarded (garrisoned) by God's power through your faith till you fully **inherit** that final salvation that is ready to be revealed for you in the last time.

Look at this blessed inheritance which He has so freely given to all those who call upon the name of the Lord to save them and to aid them, through His powerful Holy Spirit, to walk in righteousness, a gift He has given to all Believers in Christ----

Revelation 21:6-8 (TLB) ⁶ It is finished! I am the A and the Z—the Beginning and the End. I will give to the thirsty the springs of the Water of Life—as a gift! ⁷ Everyone who conquers will **inherit** all these blessings, and I will be his God and he will be my son.

Consider this—2 Peter 3:9 (TLB) ⁹ He isn't really being slow about his promised return, even though it sometimes seems that way. But he is waiting, for the good reason that he is not willing that any should perish, **and he is giving more time for sinners to repent.**

Many are familiar with the story of the Prodigal Son. Read this story of Grace for the first time, or again.

Luke 15:1-24 (AMP) ¹¹ Then He said, "A certain man had two sons. ¹² The younger of them [inappropriately] said to his father, '**Father, give**

me the share of the property that falls to me.' So he divided the estate between them. [13] A few days later, the younger son gathered together everything [that he had] and traveled to a distant country, and there he wasted his fortune in reckless *and* immoral living. [14] Now when he had spent everything, a severe famine occurred in that country, and he began to do without *and* be in need. [15] So he went and forced himself on one of the citizens of that country, who sent him into his fields to feed pigs. [16] He would have gladly eaten the [carob] pods that the pigs were eating [but they could not satisfy his hunger], and no one was giving *anything* to him.

[17] But when he [finally] came to his senses, he said, 'How many of my father's hired men have more than enough food, while I am dying here of hunger! [18] I will get up and go to my father, and I will say to him, "Father, I have sinned against heaven and in your sight. [19] I am no longer worthy to be called your son; [just] treat me like one of your hired men."' [20] So he got up and came to his father."

"But while he was still a long way off, his father saw him and was moved with compassion *for him*, and ran and embraced him and kissed him. [21] And the son said to him, 'Father, I have sinned against heaven and in your sight; I am no longer worthy to be called your son.' [22] **But the father said to his servants, 'Quickly bring out the best robe [for the guest of honor] and put it on him; and give him a ring for his hand, and sandals for his feet.** [23] And bring the fattened calf and slaughter it, and let us [invite everyone and] feast and celebrate; [24] **for this son of mine was [as good as] dead and is alive again; he was lost and has been found.'** So they began to celebrate."

Imagine this... that the God of the Universe, the Creator of all good things... will coming running to YOU, to grab you up and twirl you around in His everlasting, loving arms... for all time and for all eternity!!! What a joy!! What a divine inheritance!!! And what a legacy to pass on to your children and to all the generations to come!!!

Printed in the United States
By Bookmasters